THE SPIRITUAL HIERARCHY and THE GREAT WHITE BROTHERHOOD

"As it is written in the prophets, behold, I send my Messenger before thy face, which shall prepare thy way before thee."

(Mark 1:2)

THE SPIRITUAL HIERARCHY
and
THE GREAT WHITE BROTHERHOOD

by: JEREMIAH

THE SPIRITUAL HIERARCHY
and
THE GREAT WHITE BROTHERHOOD

Published by

THE CENTER OF UNIVERSAL TRUTH
P.O. Box 1274
Joshua Tree, CA 92252
U.S.A.

Library of Congress Catalog Card No. 3 448-425
International Standard Book No. (ISBN) 0-9639053-0-9

First printing September 1992
Second printing October 1993

CONTENTS

DEDICATION

This book is gratefully dedicated to my All-Wise, Loving Creator and also to my Elder Brothers and Sisters in Realms of Spirit...the Ascended Host and Saints robed in white raiment.

THE SPIRITUAL HIERARCHY
and
THE GREAT WHITE BROTHERHOOD

FOREWORD

Planet Earth has begun a cyclic transition into a New Cosmic Age, the Age of Aquarius, and leaving behind the Age of Pisces. Earth now enters the biblically-prophesied "*new heaven and new earth*"* to involve a New Cycle of Life-expression and a new civilization with a renovated Race of Man. This present Man-made world, this present civilization, will be dissolved into the energies from which it was manifested and new planetary conditions in the fourth dimension will prevail on Earth.

To prepare today's humanity for the incoming Cosmic Age and its New Cycle of Life-expression was this book written. For, the renovated humanity expressing as a New Race of Man in the New Age will necessarily express a different quality of consciousness, a fourth-dimensional consciousness, having abilities considered super-human in today's world.

The dissolution of this present Age of Pisces with its low-frequency negative conditions, the Kali Yuga of the Hindus (the "*Age of Darkness*"), into the higher frequencies of the Age of Aquarius, the Satya Yuga of the Hindus (the "*Age of Truth*"), will result in an Age of Enlightenment with a Christed Consciousness prevailing among the New Race of Man. The

* Isaiah 65:17; 66:12; II Peter 3:13; Revelation 21:1.

"*Priests of God and of Christ*" will be in control of all education and religion during the prophesied "*thousand years of Christ*",* while communication and commerce with Beings from other planets will be common in the New Age and its New Cycle of Life-expression.

Consequently, many human souls will attain a Spiritually-anointed, Spiritually-enlightened, Christed Consciousness during this incoming New Cosmic Cycle to thereby become as God-enlightened Saints, Prophets and Masters. Many human souls are thus expected to come forth from a humanized condition into a Spiritualized Condition and thereby cause their ascension into Realms of Spirit from whence they originated. They will consequently join their Elder Brothers and Sisters who had previously ascended and become a part of our Creator's vast Spiritual Hierarchy of Spiritual Beings inhabiting the limitless Omniverse and its many galaxies, universes, stars and planets.

* Revelation 20:4, 6.

THE SPIRITUAL HIERARCHY
and
THE GREAT WHITE BROTHERHOOD

Introduction

The author, as a Spiritual Teacher, frequently contacts and communes with his innate Source of All-Knowledge and Wisdom...his Spiritual Essence, the Father within. Through such Divine Contact and Communion with the Father, with God within his soul, was the basis of this book established.

Unfortunately, knowledge regarding Realms of Spirit is woefully inadequate or completely false in today's world. And as to where various God-enlightened Saints, Prophets and Masters are presently and what they may be doing since their Spiritual Ascension is a seeming mystery even throughout institutional religion. This book therefore explains their whereabouts and activities as being members of the Great White Brotherhood which forms a part of our Creator's vast Spiritual Hierarchy. Thus the Ultimate Destiny of every human soul can be understood from the content of this book, as compared to mere beliefs and opinions about some type of "*Heaven*" or "*Paradise*" that awaits "*good*" human souls.

Unquestionably, without adequate knowledge of Spiritual Realms of Life, any authentic and true information regarding Man's Ultimate Destiny beyond his human plane of Life could not become known except through personal

Communion with the Creator. As is apparent, the world's realm of knowledge about Man's Ultimate Destiny in Life, or about Realms of Spirit, is indeed meager and at best only of a theoretical, superficial, superstitious quality.

The content of this book is therefore founded on direct Revelation from the Creator -- the only Source of TRUE Knowledge and Wisdom -- obtained through this author's personal Communion with the Creator. Was it not from this Divine Source of True Knowledge and Wisdom that the world's Holy Writ came forth as Divine Teachings and Revelations expressed through various great Saints, Prophets and Masters? And it was this same Divine Source of True Knowledge and Wisdom that offered this author an informative Communion in response to his prayerful request for knowledge regarding the Great White Brotherhood and its relationship, if any, to the Spiritual Hierarchy of many Spiritual Beings.

Three Spiritual Communions contained herein depict Man's complete history from his original creation to his final destiny. The first Communion from the Creator explains His Original Creation as brought forth by great Spirit-Beings that manifested galaxies, universes, stars and planets throughout the Omniverse. Thereafter the creation of other Spirit-Beings, of "*Mankind*", was consummated to inhabit the planets.

The second Spiritual Communion herein was offered by the Christed Jesus bluntly stating that this world, this civilization, is a Man-made miscreation in total opposition to the Law and Will of the Creator. He further warns that this civilization, this world, is faced with a self-destruction.

In the third Spiritual Communion the Creator explains the basis of the Spiritual Hierarchy and associated Great White Brotherhood composed of millions of Angels, Archangels, Masters, Lords and Gods that dwell throughout the infinite Omniverse and its many galaxies, universes, stars and planets. The Spiritual Hierarchy, the Creator states, is Man's final destiny when regaining his original Spirituality to become as a great Ascended Master, Archangel, Lord and God...eventually as a co-Creator with Him.

This author has therefore attempted to present all facts and principles of Spiritual Reality as simply as possible and hope that current confusion, erroneous beliefs, false doctrines and even superstitions throughout mainstream religion will be dissolved as a result of the facts and principles offered in this book.

It is with deep gratitude to my Creator, my own Divine Essence, that I have been privileged to bring forth such facts and principles relating to the Original Creation and to Realms of Spirit involving the Spiritual Hierarchy and its associated Great White Brotherhood.

*　　　*　　　*

THE SPIRITUAL HIERARCHY
and
THE GREAT WHITE BROTHERHOOD

Chapter 1

Man's Ultimate Destiny

Man's Ultimate Destiny, or Cosmic Destiny, in his expression of Life is generally a mystery within the world's realm of academic and religious knowledge. Except for many inconsistent and often fallacious religious doctrines, the billions of humans in this supposedly advanced civilization do not truly know who and what they are in relation to their innate nature and True State in Life. Nor are they fully informed regarding their True Source of Beingness and where they are going in relation to their Cosmic Purpose in Life.

This Race of Man on Planet Earth has been allocated to consist of 10-billion human souls. Of this total, over 5-billion are presently embodied in the physical plane, while most of the others are discarnate in the astral plane of Life-expression. Of these 10-billion human souls that have been inhabiting this planet in their many physical embodiments, only a few thousand have attained their Ultimate Destiny of Spiritual Enlightenment and resurrection.

Ironically, some of these Spiritually-enlightened, resurrected souls had arrived from other planets or even from Realms of Spirit, as selfless volunteers, to aid and extricate Earth's humanity from its pitiful state of self-caused suffering and death. These Spiritually-enlightened souls, whether attaining their Ultimate Destiny on Earth or other planets, have been described as Masters, Lords, Avatars, Archangels and even as Gods and Goddesses by Earth's humanity. But regardless of their selfless aid and Divine Teachings offered to Earth's unenlightened souls, the billions of these yet Earth-bound souls have repeatedly experienced many cycles of physical births and deaths. Although millions of years have elapsed since their descent, separation and degeneration from their original Spiritualized Expression as the Creator's Image and Likeness -- involving numerous human embodiments in various civilizations -- these degenerated souls stubbornly continue to remain in slumber regarding their True State in Life as immortal Spiritual Beings.

Why, despite many Spiritual Teachings and Revelations offered Earth's humanity throughout the Ages, does the average human remain hypnotized by this illusory world of gross materialism, sensualism and uncountable false gods? The basic reason is that various Teachings and Revelations yet existing from the past, usually called Scriptures, whether Oriental or Occidental, have been either ignored or adulterated. As had occurred in past, now-dead civilizations of Man's long history on Earth, transcendent Teachings offered by God-enlightened Beings have been and still continue to be mistranslated or misinterpreted by their followers, or even purposely distorted by unscrupulous authorities so as to increase their prestige and power.

It is no different in today's civilization. TRUE religion has become seriously adulterated and thereby institutionalized and divided into many sects, denominations and cults founded on uncountable beliefs, doctrines, dogmas and hallowed traditions. Certainly, if Spiritual Teachings remained in their original purity and also correctly interpreted and taught, then many more human souls could attain Spiritual Enlightenment and resulting resurrection from further physical deaths.

It is therefore a clear-cut case of TRUE religion having been stripped of its Spirituality to become but a dogma of literal words, pretentious rituals and hallowed traditions. For, the word "*religion*", derived from the Latin "*religio*" has a deeper meaning than popularly believed...it is correctly defined: "*to unite; to bind together*". Consequently it is through foundational principles of TRUE religion that a human soul should be given appropriate teaching and guidance to unite it and bind it with its Spiritual Essence, the Spirit of God within the soul.

Since such teaching and guidance has not been given the masses by institutionalized religion, the billions of human souls inhabiting this planet therefore slumber deeply in dreams of their Earth-bound egos and senses. Significantly, in regard to Man's genesis on this planet, the word "*shenah*" which described and related to conditions and time-periods of human history in the original Chaldean version of the Bible is correctly defined as "*sleep; dream; changes*". However, the Old Testament writers of Man's genesis mistranslated this ancient Chaldean word "*shenah*" as "*years*".*

Due to such mistranslation, biblical scholars and clerics have been relating Man's genesis on Earth as beginning some 8,000 years ago. However, the "*years*" they related to Adam, Seth, Enos, Cainan, Mahalaleel, Jared, Enoch, Methuselah, Lamech and Noah had each covered long periods of great changes and mutations on Earth, actually involving many Cosmic Ages and Cycles. For, these biblical names not only represent, in some cases, important Spiritual Beings, but also relate to and describe the quality of humanity's mass-conciousness and its various civilizations that existed during those eras.

Man has therefore inhabited this planet for many millions of years, as has been revealed by archaelogical discoveries of bones and fossils that now extend human history to about 10-million years. Moreover, that Chaldean word "shenah" also informs us that Man -- originally a pristine Spiritual Being -- has been in a "*dream-state*"...SLEEPING to his True

* Refer to the AQUARIAN REVELATION, by this writer, for the original Chaldean version -- the Sapher Torah -- of Man's genesis on Earth.

State in Life during these long periods of earthly changes and associated mutations of animals and other Life-forms.

It is a pathetic situation that due to serious mistranslations in the Bible neither Christianity or Judaism is raising human souls into Oneness with God. Ironically, the Judaic-Christian Bible, though originally written by various humans and then translated into different languages by other humans, is yet believed by many religionists as being the pure "*Word of God*". Regardless of probable mistranslations by various scribes, priests, translators and theologians over the centuries, the Bible is revered to a greater extent than a direct Spiritual Teaching or Revelation from God, if brought forth by a God-enlightened Prophet or Master of today.

And as the Bible being the actual Word of God, it must be realized that much of the Old Testament merely describes historical experiences of the Jewish people; moreover, much of the New Testament contains various activities of Jesus and his disciples...neither of which are profound Spiritual Teachings directly from God.

Furthermore, since each of the biblical Testaments originated during separate eras and also written in different languages -- the Old Testament in the now-dead Chaldean language and the New Testament in the now-dead Aramaic language -- the resulting translations and interpretations have caused many variations in today's languages. Consequently both

Chapter 1

Christianity and Judaism are seriously divided with many sects, denominations and cults. Additionally each of these many sects, denominations and cults have conceived their own theology involving various types of doctrines, creeds, dogmas, rituals, sacraments and even hallowed traditions as their form of religion.

Therefore TRUE religion, as PURE Spiritual Truth from God, is generally nonexistent in today's world. This is clearly evident in the pitiful state of Earth's humanity not being able to achieve their True State in Life of Oneness with God, the Spirit of God within their souls. The inconsistent and misleading Man-conceived religions make it very difficult, if not impossible, for human souls to attain the exalted state of Oneness with their innate God-Presence described by God-enlightened Prophets and Masters as Kingdom of God, Secret Place of the Most High, Nirvana and other names. Today, Oneness with God is described by a few teachers of Spiritual Truth as Christ-Consciousness, Buddha-Consciousness, Krishna-Consciousness, Cosmic-Consciousness and God-Consciousness.

* * *

Chapter 2

The Original Creation

Unfortunately, present religious Scriptures are generally but remnants or mistranslations of original Spiritual Teachings offered by God-enlightened Prophets, Masters, Swamis and Avatars thousands of years ago. Offered in ancient, now-dead languages these Teachings have been translated and also mistranslated into other languages from century to century. Thereafter they have been interpreted and also misinterpreted by various scribes, clerics and theologians.

As an example, the story of Creation as written in the Book of Genesis is mainly an allegory, generally but a symbolic story brought forth by a Jewish mystic some time during the 2nd-century B.C. after the Jews were freed from their Babylonian captivity. Because the original story of Creation was initially offered in the Chaldean language, offered to the Patriarch Abraham (a Chaldean) by the great Ascended Master Melchizedek, consequently the Jewish mystic, unable to translate the then-dead Chaldean language, was forced to write the story of Creation in an allegorical, symbolic manner.

Consequently, in his "translation" from the dead Chaldean language, as originally written by Abraham in the 19th-century B.C., this Jewish mystic wrote the story of Creation in a simplified, elementary manner in accord with his understanding and ability to translate the original Chaldean text named the Sapher Torah. He thus used symbolic words and names such as "*Adam*" and "*Hawwah*" having meanings in the Hebrew language but not factual in regard to the original principles of Creation. Nor was he able to explain that the creation of Man, of Planet Earth and of other planets, plus stars, universes and galaxies throughout the limitless Omniverse had been completed many billions of Earth-years ago and not in a symbolic "*seven days*".*

Due to erroneous translation of the original Creation, plus varying interpretations, doctrines and beliefs regarding Man's genesis, Earth's humanity is therefore in a state of much confusion and division regarding its beginnings. This confusion and division has been greatly increased as a result of scientific theories that Man has evolved from a primordial state, seemingly evolving from an amoeba into an ape-like condition over billions of years. And that from this ape-like condition then developed into a more-intelligent humanoid state.

However, strongly opposing these *scientific* theories, religious people, described as "*Creationists*", have used their biblical story of

* For the factual story of Creation, including actual facts about the "great flood" of Noah's time, refer to the Aquarian Revelation published by the Center of Universal Truth.

Genesis to prove their *truth* of Man's creation as originating from two humans called Adam and Eve. And according to their interpretation of historical events and of Ages related to various individuals recorded in the present-day Book of Genesis, as brought forth by the Jewish mystic and later writers, that creation of this planet and of Man occurred about 8,000 years ago. Consequently, a continual stream of controversy and criticism has ensued between such Bible-believers and of material-minded scientists described as "*Evolutionists*". And to support their theories, these Evolutionists have been attempting to prove that "*the first living organisms began via ordinary physical and chemical processes, therefore that the past and present diversity of plants and animals is the result of natural selection operating on natural genetic variability over thousands or millions of years*".*

However, regardless of the Creationists' deep convictions about Man's genesis according to the biblical account of Creation, and the Evolutionists believing that Man evolved from an amoeba, the actual facts refute both the religious beliefs and the scientific theories. For, to repeat, the biblical account of Creation, including Man's genesis, was but an allegory, a symbolic story, written by a Jewish mystic due to his inability to translate the original Chaldean text as given to the Patriarch Abraham by the Ascended Master Melchizedek.

* Quoted from scientific lectures, symposiums and journals.

Chapter 2

Comparably, however, scientific theories are merely founded on Mankind's current sciences as biology, geology, astronomy, chemistry and physics, the basis of which are each composed of energy. Because energy is never static, always in motion and vibration, therefore the basis of these sciences -- as they exist today -- did not exist in past times of Earth's long history. In fact, many earthly changes, variations in Nature, geologic cataclysms, plus astronomical changes of nearby planets and stars have occurred during past millenia. Therefore what exists on and around Planet Earth today has been changed, destroyed or buried by great earth-quakes, floods, land-slides, sunken continents (such as Atlantis and Mu), plus the catastrophic tipping of Earth's axis during the Pleistocene Epoch about 4-million years ago, thus resulting in the "*ice ages*".

Quite apparently, any "*big-bang*" theory regarding the original creation of this planet, plus its neighboring planets and stars, as well as this entire galaxy of thousands of other planets and stars is but an assumption of earth-bound human minds not having a Cosmic-oriented consciousness. A Cosmic-oriented consciousness would encompass ALL aspects and parts of Creation, beginning from the FOUNDATIONAL PRINCIPLE of the Creative Force, then to the various octaves of energy, and finally to the multitudinous creations and manifestations throughout the limitless Omniverse of many galaxies, universes, stars and planets.

The Original Creation

This Creative Force, described in many ways by worldly religions as God, Creator, Allah, Brahman, Yahweh, Lord and other names, has within ItSelf various transcendent Attributes and Powers that apparently defy even the greatest philosophers and scientists on Earth. For, this Creative Force has created from within ItSelf the many octaves of intelligent energies, then from these energies manifested many galaxies each containing uncountable planets, stars and moons. Furthermore, on each of these planets the energies were also utilized to create millions of various types of physical, material, organic and inorganic manifestations ranging from simple amoebas, to uncountable forms of vegetation, insects, fish, birds and animals.

An intelligent thinker can quickly recognize that every type of vegetation and every living creation in Earth's waters or its land areas has within itself a definite expression of Life-Force and Intelligence. In fact, the very energy of which these manifestations are formed, the basic electrons and atoms of which they are composed, have an inherent Life-Force and Intelligence within the electrons and atoms that CAUSED these innumerable manifestations to become formed and materialized into vegetation, insects, fish, birds and animals. For, it is evident that each of these materialized forms, whether in the category of vegetation such as a carrot, a tree, a melon, a bush, a nut, a flower, or any other form of the thousands of various types of vegetation, each has within itself an inherent Life-Force and Intelligence. And each is also capable of reproducing itself through its own self-created seeds.

And it is no different in regard to all other forms of Creation, whether insects, fish, birds or animals. Each expresses an inherent Life-Force and Intelligence. This inherent Intelligence has been called by science, for want of a more appropriate name, as "*instinct*". The expression of both the Life-Force and Intelligence within each of the millions of these forms of Life is expressed according to its intended purpose and need on this planet as decreed by the omnipresent Source of ALL Life and Intelligence. This omnipresent Source of ALL Life and Intelligence is generally described by enlightened thinkers as the Creator. Religions around the world have called the Creator as God, Allah, Brahman, Lord, Yahweh, Tao and other names. This planet therefore contains innumerable forms of creation which Mankind relates as a "*balance of Nature*". And as a result of this balance of Nature throughout these many forms of Life and Intelligence, each created-form fulfills a certain purpose or need for another created-form... which causes this planet to be a completely self-sufficient Unit unto itself while floating and orbitting in seemingly empty space millions of miles from the sun and neighboring planets.

And what of Man? How did he come forth? Was he a special Creation brought forth by the omnipresent Source of all Life and Intelligence, created as the Image and Likeness of this Source called God, as stated biblically? Or was he but a humanoid that had evolved from an ape-like state as theorized by many scientists? However, even the biblical version of Man's genesis on Earth is somewhat confusing because the 1st chapter in the Book of Genesis states that he was originally created by God as His Image and Likeness, but the 2nd chapter states that he was created *"OF the dust of the ground by a Lord God"*.* This symbolic story of Man's creation, as written by the Jewish mystic, has thus baffled and divided many Creationists as to whether Man is truly the Image and Likeness of God's Spirit and therefore essentially a Spiritual Being in a human body...or, is he but a special Life-form created from Earth's dust of the ground that became a Homo sapien, an Adam/ Eve Being?

To explain and clarify the confusion and apparent contradictions among the religious Creationists and the scientific Evolutionists regarding Man's actual genesis, a personal Communication, a Divine Communion, with the Creator is herein offered. Recorded verbatim in a conscious and vocal manner by this author, it contains actual facts of the original Creation and of Man's genesis prior to his habitation on Earth...offered directly by the Creator, the Source of ALL Life and Intelligence throughout the infinite Omniverse with its many galaxies, universes, stars and planets.

* Genesis 1:27 & 2:7.

Chapter 2

The Communion from our Creator:

"A good morning to you, My beloved son! Thank you for joining Me in this Communion, a Communion that you had desired and, as a consequence, I AM responding to your desire. And in regard to this desire, in regard to the subject for this Communion, it is due to a question that you have. And it relates to the Original Creation.

"This, of course, is a very important subject and certainly interesting. And it will be of value to many others. And when offered in a Lesson, or Discourse, or Class to others, it is of course necessary, My beloved son, that you do understand the principle of the Original Creation, yes, the actual facts...because the present records, the present Scriptures are not very accurate, yes, misleading.

"And so, let Us understand this actuality in relation to the Original Creation. This, of course, would relate to the Period when there was, shall We say, nothing throughout My Omniverse when -- as it is stated biblically -- there was a "great void". In this regard, My beloved son, this could be related as a fact, because without any Creation, without any of the galaxies, universes, stars and planets, there was, We might say, great emptiness in and throughout the Omniverse.

"And, what actually did exist? Did I Exist? Yes, My beloved son, I did Exist. I did, My beloved son, Express. In other words, the Consciousness that I AM, this Spirit that I AM was in Expression. And yet, My beloved son, this Expression of Mine was in a

quiescent State, in a rather dormant State.

"And, what occurred initially? Well, initially, My beloved son, I began to Express, I began to become more Expressive. And consequently, I brought forth from My Beingness -- the Consciousness, the Spirit that I AM -- My Progeny. And this Progeny, of course, is My Image and Likeness.

"And this Progeny, originally, My son, was capable of Expressing Me in quite a complete manner and, consequently, was capable of bringing forth the energies that were necessary so that a creation, a manifestation from energies was to be possible. So, consequently, this Progeny, this Image and Likeness -- actually great Spirit-Beings -- brought forth, in accord with My Will and of course with application of My Law, the various energies that would be necessary to bring forth and manifest various forms of Creation.

"And so, this was initiated in such manner. And these great Spirits consequently began to bring forth, to manifest planetary systems. And from these planetary systems came forth galaxies. And thus, initially, a galaxy was formed here with planetary systems, or universes, and another galaxy there with planetary systems or universes.

"And from that point, My son, I then began to bring forth increasing numbers of other forms of Progeny...that is, more of My Image and Likeness. And these were to inhabit these planetary systems, these various planets. And these Progeny, My son, were those such as YOU. And consequently they were offered the opportunity to inhabit any of these planets

that had been previously manifested by these great Spirits.

"And so, gradually, you and other Spirit-Beings began to inhabit these planets and, as a consequence, began to have experiences and consequent knowledge and understnding in regard to inhabiting a planet, in regard to being a part of that which is material. And consequently, you brought forth physical bodies. And in these physical bodies, unfortunately, became increasingly humanized, increasingly material-minded, earth-minded... and, as a consequence, caused your self to be in a humanized, earth-bound and material consciousness for many many Ages, yes, many Cosmic Ages and, in fact, many Cosmic Cycles.

"And those of you who are awakening to the Truth of your Beingness -- that you are actually Spirit-Beings -- are coming forth, gradually, out of this dream-state and realizing that you are actually Spirit-Beings...and, as a result, coming forth much wiser and stronger as Masters. And thus, as Masters, to ascend and to be creative. Yes, to be sufficiently creative as My co-Creators and somewhat, shall We say, somewhat similar to these great Spirit-Beings who were originally brought forth from My Beingness.

"And thus, it is stated biblically that they desired that you be like them. You were brought forth, initially, as My Image and Likeness, and they desired that you would become as they are...as great Creators of planetary systems and galaxies.

"And thus, My beloved son, My Creation is

expanding...it has been expanding as a result of increasing Beings becoming ascended from an earthly or human condition, and consequently, becoming as great Masters, and as great Lords, and as great Gods, and My co-Creators throughout My infinite Omniverse.

"And in this regard, My beloved son, you are, shall We say, graduating from a humanized, earthly condition and now becoming an Ascended Master...and to become as a great Lord, and God, and a great co-Creator with Me in My infinite Omniverse.

"Thank you, My beloved son, for coming to Me and, especially, for arising, for ascending into My Realms of Spirit into a complete Oneness with Me...again!"

It is hoped, it is intended, that this chapter and above Communion from our Creator, in fact this entire book, will bring forth a change-over, a re-direction, a transformation in Mankind's mass-consciousness. The prevailing beliefs, the philosophies, ideologies and theologies in this seemingly advanced civilization are yet limiting human souls to not even recognize that Man is not alone in this vast Omniverse, that other Races of Man and great Spiritual Beings inhabit the many planets and stars created for their use and expression of Life and Consciousness. Ironically, even visitations of and personal contacts with extra-terrestrial Beings and their space-crafts have been censored by governments and by religions, while Man is depicted by schools and museum displays as crawling forth from a fish-like state onto dry land and evolving into an ape-like body.

This entire world is thus founded on gross ignorance of Man's TRUE Nature as a Spiritual Being having potentials of expressing his Creator's Spirit from within his soul. And as a Spiritual Being capable of expressing his Creator's Spirit, Man is therefore as limitless as is the Creator...for, Man is the Creator's Spiritual Progeny, the Creator's Spiritual Image and Likeness, the Temple of God in human form.

* * *

THE SPIRITUAL HIERARCHY
and
THE GREAT WHITE BROTHERHOOD

Chapter 3

Spiritual Ascensions Rare

As apparent throughout the world, Mankind's True State in Life as a Spiritual Being is generally a mystery even within the realm of religion. That a human soul has the opportunity to experience a rapturous Spiritual Ascension prior to death of its physical body is almost unheard of in today's world. The many sectarian doctrines, creeds, dogmas preached by orthodox and fundamental religions do not even clarify that a human can become regenerated to his original condition as a Spiritual Being prior to a physical death.

A rapturous Spiritual Ascension therefore awaits you. You came forth from Realms of Spirit and into them shall you return. Essentially a Spiritual Being and not a human, you must become again what you were originally. Eventually you must be "*born again*" to regain your original condition as a glorious Angelic Being expressing immortal Life in company with other immortal Beings in the Creator's vast Spiritual Hierarchy inhabiting the infinite Omniverse and its many galaxies, universes, stars and planets. As God's Spiritual Image and Likeness all is necessary is to realize your TRUE Self and thereby cause an exalted State of Life-expression in Realms of Spirit as an immortal, infinite Ascended Being.

Unfortunately, in contrast to billions of Earth-bound humans that sleep to their True State in Life, a relatively few had achieved this exalted State in Life to become as Ascended Beings. Attaining Oneness with their God-Essence and described by humanity as super-human Prophets, Masters, Lords and other titles, they now express their Divine Heritage in Realms of Spirit. Having achieved a regenerated, resurrected state of Life-expression in which they originally existed prior to their degeneration into a humanized condition, these now-Spiritualized Souls are now immortal and limitless.

No longer as finite humans in earthly bondage, such Spiritualized Souls now express Life and Consciousness in any Realm, Plane or Dimension of the infinite Omniverse. Their Oneness and conscious Attunement, their At-Onement, with their God-Essence permits them to enter any aspect or level of Creation throughout the limitless Omniverse of many galaxies, universes, stars and planets. As Spiritual Beings they are capable of limitless, eternal expression of Life and Consciousness as an inseparable, integral part of the Creator's omnipresent Spirit. As stated biblically, each Being personally experiences "*All that the Father hath is thine*", "*...in the many Mansions of the Father's House*".

These Spiritual Beings, formerly humans in corporeal bodies, now express the Infinite

Wisdom, Universal Love, Cosmic Power, Eternal Life and other Attributes of our omnipresent Creator...called Father, Allah, God, Brahman, Lord, Jehovah and other names by Earth's humanity. Since the Creator is Spirit and Spirit is Consciousness -- an omnipresent, immanent, all-pervading Spirit or Consciousness* -- therefore His Individualized Expressions have the inherent ability to express and apply all of His Attributes and Qualities. In other words, the Individualized Expressions of the Creator are Individualized Spirits of the Creator's All-Spirit, Spirit-Beings expressing the Life and Consciousness of their omnipresent Creator. And these Individualized Spirits of the Creator's All-Spirit are truly His Image and Likeness, biblically described as "*Man*".

Since all humanity, or "*Man*", was originally created in the Spiritual Image and Likeness of the Creator-God, therefore this includes you. And just as Spirit-Beings are an integral, inseparable part of the Creator's omnipresent Spirit, so you are also. Therefore, just as you now exist and physically express in the atmosphere of this planet, so you exist physically, mentally, emotionally and Spiritually in the All-Spirit and All-Consciousness of your omnipresent Creator. To quote St. Paul "*In Him we live, and move, and have our Being*".**

* To understand ancient Scriptures in a deeper manner, substitute the word "*Spirit*" with "Consciousness", or when the Sanskrit word "Atma" appears. ** Acts 17:28.

Chapter 3

As the Individualized Expression of your Creator's All-Spirit and All-Consciousness, you therefore express the Life, Consciousness, Intelligence and other Attributes of your Creator... but in a limited, restricted, finite manner. "*Ye are the Temple of God and the Spirit of God dwelleth in you*"*...but this human Temple, your personality-self, subjugates and obstructs the Spirit of God from Its fullest Expression.

While God-enlightened Beings in Realms of Spirit are capable of expressing Life continually in an immortal, deathless state, you are probably prone to experience a death of your human body. And while these God-enlightened Beings are capable of expressing the Creator's All-Consciousness in the form of Transcendent Knowledge and Cosmic Wisdom, you are presently limited to only a human level of consciousness merely expressing the world's questionable, mundane knowledge.

Simply, the difference between God-enlightened Prophets, Masters and Ascended Spirit-Beings -- compared to typical, earthly humans -- is that such God-enlightened Beings have attained their original Oneness with their God-Essence and experienced consequent resurrection into Man's True State in Life, while typical humans are yet enthralled, entangled and in bondage to their fallen, degenerated state as corporeal Beings. And yet, for any human to become an immortal Spirit-Being, it is only

* I Corinthians 3:16.

necessary for that human to free himself/herself from earthly and worldly bondage to thereby become God-enlightened and Spiritualized.

To repeat, ye are the Temple of God and the Spirit of God dwelleth in you. It is therefore only necessary to transcend this human Temple, this personality-self and physical body, and consequently permit the Spirit of God to become expressive. When the Spirit of God is released into expression throughout the personality-self and physical body the total human Temple becomes Spiritualized and God-enlightened. As a consequence that personality-self and Temple then expresses on Earth as a God-enlightened Saint, Prophet or Master.

*   *   *

Chapter 4

The Seven Rays

It should be clearly understood that the Creator is Spirit, an omnipresent, all-pervading Spirit. Though not visible to human vision, Spirit can be perceived when a human consciousness is God-enlightened to become as a great Saint, Prophet or Master. Through such enlightenment the Creator can then be seen as Light, as Spiritual Light. This Spiritual Light, though not seen by typical human vision is, however, being recognized by Earth's scientists -- in but a very limited manner -- described as "*Cosmic Rays*", or as "*ultra-gamma rays*". Measured with instruments fabricated from earthly elements, the full scope of Spiritual Light is however impossible to detect with such scientific instruments...in fact, only the lowest frequency of this Light can be detected, of which there are seven basic frequencies or Seven Rays.

As clearly stated in the world's Holy Writ, the Creator is Spirit and this Spirit is Light...Spiritual Light.* Therefore it is initially necessary to recognize that the basis, the fundamental principle of the Seven Rays is the

* "...God is Light and in Him is no darkness at all." (I John 1:5) Also see Isaiah 60:20; Matthew 7:8; Revelation 22:5.

Spiritual Light of the Creator, whether He is described by humanity as God, Brahman, Allah, Yahweh, Lord or other names. And this Spiritual Light composes Seven Rays which bring forth, manifest, all physical and material forms of Creation.

To repeat, the Creator, though generally described as Spirit, is actually Pure Light, Pure Crystal-clear Light. No, not the electronic light of the Sun, for this is a yellowish, golden light composed of electrons, of electronic light, which is only an expression, a manifestation of the Pure Crystal-clear Light of the Creator.

The Pure Crystal-clear Light of the Creator is initially reduced in its Purity or, as commonly stated, is "*refracted*" into seven colors. This refraction into seven colors is also brought forth from the light of our Sun, thus creating the spectrum of seven colors. For example, when Sunlight is reduced in its intensity and refracted through clouds we then describe this refraction into colors as a "*rainbow*". Such refraction of Sunlight is also accomplished through a glass prism which breaks down the vibratory frequency of Sunlight into the lower frequencies of colors.

So, these Seven Rays are actually composed of the spectrum of seven colors. These Seven Rays of colors are therefore as Seven Radiations of vibratory frequencies. And since the Creator is omnipresent and all-pervading throughout the limitless Omniverse, consequently His Pure Spirit and Pure Light is also omnipresent and all-pervading. Therefore, the Seven Rays, as Seven Radiations of vibratory frequencies composing the color-spectrum, are also omnipresent and all-pervading throughout the Omniverse of many galaxies, universes, stars and planets.

Now, it is important to understand that the Seven Rays, or Radiations, are the Seven Attributes of the Creator's Consciousness and Beingness in Expression throughout all Creation. This means that the Spirit of the Creator, as Pure Crystal-clear Light, is also the Consciousness and Beingness of the Creator in Expression. Thus, the Seven Radiations, or Rays, are the Seven Foundational Attributes and Qualities of the Creator being expressed and radiated throughout the Omniverse. And it is therefore from these Seven Radiations of the Creator's omnipresent Spirit and Consciousness that all of Creation is manifested. This was symbolized in the biblical story of Creation as requiring "*seven days*".

Stated in a more technical manner, the Pure Crystal-clear Light of the Creator is first refracted or stepped-down from Its Pure Spiritual Frequency into Seven Radiations of lower frequencies as Seven Cosmic Rays which correlate with the color-spectrum. Although these Seven Cosmic Rays are not seen by human vision however, as previously stated, they have been recorded by scientific instruments -- but only in an elementary manner -- and described as "*Cosmic Rays*" and as "*ultra-gamma rays*".

Secondly, these ultra-high frequencies of the Creator's Seven Attributes, radiated throughout the Omniverse as Seven Rays, are then stepped-down in their vibratory frequency into the electromagnetic energies -- the electrons and atoms -- which are now becoming understood by scientists.

The electromagnetic energies thus permeate the entire Omniverse, being as stepped-down frequencies of the Creator's omnipresent Consciousness of Spiritual Light and associated Seven Radiations. Then from the electromagnetic energies are all forms of Creation manifested into visible, tangible things...ranging from pure electrons concentrated as the electronic light of our Sun and down into denser, grosser forms as animals, vegetation and minerals.

Consequently, it can now be more readily understood that all forms of Creation -- and also all forms of Life and Consciousness -- are immersed in and an integral part of the Creator's Seven Radiations. And thus an inseparable expression of the omnipresent Spirit and Consciousness of the Creator. As a consequence, not only is every form of manifested Creation composed of the same electromagnetic energy which is a stepped-down force and power from the Seven Radiations, but every form of Creation also expresses certain degrees of the Creator's omnipresent Spirit and Consciousness, every form of Creation also expresses His Seven Attributes in various levels and qualities.

Since the Creator's omnipresent Spirit and Consciousness expresses His Seven Attributes as the Seven Radiations of Spiritual Frequencies, and these are stepped-down into lower frequencies of energy, therefore the expression of Life, the Life-Force, is also an effect of the Creator's Attributes. Thus, Life is apparent in all animated forms such as animals, birds, insects, fish and, of course, humans. Furthermore, the omnipresent Consciousness of the Creator is also apparent in all Life-forms as intelligence and feelings.

The expression of intelligence and feelings, it can be noted, varies in level and quality among the many species of animals, birds, insects and fish...yet each expresses a certain degree of intelligence and feelings as "*instinct*". This instinctive faculty in all lower Life-forms is actually a stepped-down expression of the Creator's Attribute of Wisdom, His Omniscience, that is radiated in varying levels and qualities. And each type or specie of Life-form expresses in and partakes of a specific level and quality of the Creator's Omniscience to which it is attuned from within its particular consciousness. In other words, each Life-form has its own type of DNA molecules within its body which are established at a definite vibratory frequency and thus to be attuned with, as antennas and radio receivers, to the particular level and quality of intelligence it has been created to express.

Man, in contrast, is not limited to any specific vibratory frequency in the Creator's infinite Realms of Intelligence. As the Image and Likeness of his Creator, Man therefore is the INDIVIDUALIZED EXPRESSION of the Creator's Spirit and Consciousness. Although he has subjugated his innate Spirituality by succumbing to a humanized condition in his self-created bondage to a physical-material expression of Life, yet he always has the distinct privilege to express his innate Spiritual Consciousness... whenever he so chooses to regain his original Oneness with his Creator. While the lower Life-forms remain limited to their particular level and quality of intelligence -- which is restricted to only vibratory frequencies within the psychic plane -- Man has the exclusive ability and potential to extend and attune his human mind and consciousness beyond the psychic plane into Realms of Spirit. For, of all Life-forms, only Man is a complete Spiritual Image and Expression of the infinite Creator.

Man, therefore, has all Attributes and Qualities of the Creator within his Being. But they are lying dormant within his soul and can be expressed as was possible in the beginning, prior to his descent and degeneration into an earth-bound Being. All is necessary is for Man to realize his true identity as a Spiritual Being and thereby re-establish and re-harmonize himself with the Spiritual Essence of his Beingness. In such manner does he experience

Chapter 4

Spiritual Enlightenment, the Moksha and Nirvana of Hindus and Buddhists, whereby the Pure Spiritual Light of God within his soul radiates throughout his entire body and surrounding aura. He thus experiences a Transfiguration, a complete Spiritual Transmutation described by Jesus as the Kingdom of God. Of course, a consistent dedication to one's Spiritual Essence, the God-Light within, is mandatory...which was stated by Jesus in these words: "*If thine eye be single, thy whole body shall be full of Light*".*

When Man experiences Spiritual Enlightenment he thus begins his original state of Oneness with his Spiritual Essence, his innate God-Essence, and consequently expresses his long-dormant Attributes of God. Expressing in this state of Oneness with God, he thereby expresses Life and Consciousness in the Kingdom of God...which is actually a State of Godhood, of expressing God on Earth as a Prophet or Master. As a Prophet or Master he is capable of superhuman abilities and powers relating to transcendent wisdom and great works, so-called miracles. As an effect of his Enlightenment, the Pure Light of God now radiates throughout his mind, soul and body which then expresses the Creator's Attributes and Qualities. Therefore, a God-enlightened Prophet or Master is capable of expressing the Creator's Infinite Wisdom, Universal Love,

* Matthew 6:22.

Cosmic Power and other Attributes as a natural effect of Oneness with his innate Divinity, his God-Essence.

Consequently, as a result of Enlightenment, Man now expresses God from within his Being. This involves the expression of the Creator's Seven Foundational Attributes, of which the three primary, principal Attributes are Wisdom, Love and Power. Since the Creator is Pure Spiritual Light, Man's Enlightenment causes the Creator's Light to radiate throughout Man's Being and also refracted and expressed from his consciousness in the form of the Creator's Seven Rays or Radiations, the seven colors of the spectrum, resulting from a refraction or division of the Creator's Spiritual Light. Thus, Spiritually-enlightened Man becomes capable of expressing the Creator's Seven Attributes and also emanates the Seven Radiations around his body as beautiful auric colors.

Furthermore, since Man is the Creator's Individualized Image and Likeness, the Temple of God, he also contains within himself seven Spiritual Centers...the symbolic "*seven lamps*" and "*seven candlesticks*" of the Bible.* Described as "*chakras*" in Sanskrit, these Spiritual Centers serve to qualify the Creator's Light as reflectors, or force-centers, which God-enlightened Prophets and Masters can utilize for various requirements. For example, one of these Spiritual Centers can be used by God-

* Exodus 25:31; Revelation 1:12-13 and 2:5.

enlightened Man to qualify and extend Spiritual Light as a powerful laser-beam to heal another human body or to even disintegrate an approaching bullet or nuclear missile. Furthermore, the other Centers within Man are capable of radiating the required force to levitate his body, transporting himself to any area on Earth, causing his body to be invisible to human vision and many other abilities considered by Earth-bound humanity as superhuman and as miracles.

To repeat, as the Temple of God, as the Individualized Expression of the Creator in a human form, Man has within his Being all Attributes and Qualities of his Infinite Creator. As a consequence, those men and women who attained their natural state of Oneness with their God-Essence have usually been revered as Gods and Goddesses by average humans. And so-called "*fables*" regarding "*flying carpets*" and "*Alladin and the magic lamp*" are actually symbolic stories of Man's ability to transport himself through the atmosphere (termed "*teleportation*") and also indicating his innate God-Powers symbolized in the "*magic lamp*" involving a "*Genie*", an etheric Being of Light, that performs superhuman accomplishments.

Since Man is a direct Individualization of the Creator's Spiritual Light, therefore Spiritual Light is not only radiated as the Seven Radiations of the color spectrum throughout Man's Being but also expressed as energy throughout his physical, etheric and psychic aspects. For, all Creation, all that exists is an effect of and a creation from Spirit. As a consequence, all energies are an effect of stepped-down frequencies of the Seven Radiations. Furthermore, all physical and material forms are an effect of, a manifestation of stepped-down frequencies of energy, of atoms.

Consequently, each of the Seven Radiations are stepped-down in their vibratory frequency into seven basic ranges of energy, and then these seven basic ranges of energy become the foundation for all visible and invisible forms of Creation. Thus, various combinations of electro-magnetic energy -- of atoms, the "*building blocks of the universe*" -- bring forth the many types of gases, chemicals, minerals, vegetation and animated Life-forms. Meanwhile, energies of higher vibrations (of short wave-lengths) form the realm of so-called radio frequencies, others forming the etheric and astral range of energies, and other energies that form the range of psychic frequencies.

As the Individualization of the Creator, Man, to repeat, is a complete Expression of all Attributes and Qualities of his Creator. Furthermore, Man is also a complete Unit of All-Creation, a complete Being having every Aspect of Creation composing his Beingness. Whether the Creator's Seven Attributes and corresponding Seven Radiations, which are co-ordinated with Man's seven Spiritual Centers, or the various forms and frequencies of energy, Man is composed of every Aspect of his

Creator and also of every Aspect of the visible and invisible Creation in his expression of Life, Consciousness and Beingness. Consequently, his human expression on Earth is also composed of seven Aspects...consisting of four lower bodies and three higher expressions, a total of seven Aspects upon which All-Creation is also founded.

The highest Aspect of Man's Beingness is, of course, his Spiritual Essence, his Creator's Individualized Expression of Life and Consciousness. His next lower Aspects are those two which compose his psychic expression, his mind and his soul, thus forming the basis of his human consciousness. Then, as the effect of his two psychic Aspects, through expression of thoughts and emotions from his mind and soul, he has formed mental and emotional bodies. And as the effect of the contents of these mental and emotional bodies, an etheric, astral body was manifested. And as a visible counterpart of this astral body, a denser physical body is the grossest manifestation of Man's human expression on Earth.

Man's seven Aspects of Beingness on this planet are thus composed of the seven ranges of energy, plus the Seven Radiations and corresponding Attributes of the Creator's omnipresent Spirit. The physical, earthly body of Man is composed of electromagnetic energy, of atoms, in a solidified form; and its etheric counterpart, the astral body, is also composed of electromagnetic energy but of a higher frequency and thus not solidified. Then his mental and emotional bodies -- the product of his thoughts, imaginings, desires, emotions, feelings -- consist of psychic energy (so-called "*thought-forms*" and "*brain-waves*"). Psychic energy is composed of high-frequency electrons emanated from Man's mind and soul which permeates his physical and astral bodies and also his surrounding aura.

These four lower bodies -- physical, astral, mental and emotional -- are then superseded by Man's higher Aspects, the mind and soul, the psyche or consciousness of his human expression. However, the mind and soul are not of Pure Spirit. The mind and soul are a lower, inferior expression of Man's Spiritual Essence and therefore also composed of psychic energy, but of ultra-high-frequency electrons as compared to the lower frequencies which are emanated as thoughts and emotions. From the thoughts and emotions are then produced the mental-emotional bodies resulting from Man's expressions of his mind and soul.

It should now be apparent that the humanized Image and Likeness of God, called "*Man*", in having all Attributes and Qualities of his Creator as the Essence of his Beingness, has the innate ability to control and manipulate all energies of which his human Aspects are manifested. By proper use of his mind and soul to only express thoughts, images, desires, emotions and feelings of a lofty, Spiritual Quality the resulting psychic energies which are emanated will raise the vibratory frequency of each of his four lower bodies. For, it is only logical and also quite apparent that negative, carnal, earthly, materialistic thoughts, desires, feelings, etc. of the average human cause his or her entire Beingness to remain in low and negative vibratory frequencies which manifest corresponding conditions such as various problems, illnesses and eventual death of the human personality.

However, as the Spiritual Image and Likeness of God, Man is not subjected to any negative conditions. For, Man's mind and soul, his human consciousness, has the innate ability to Spiritualize his total Beingness by simply concentrating on his Spiritual Essence. As a consequence to bring forth the Light of God to radiate in and through all seven Aspects of his Beingness. In other words, by concentrating and meditating upon the Spiritual Light, the Christ Light located at his heart, then the ultra-high Spiritual Frequencies of this Light of God within Man will stimulate and accelerate the vibratory frequencies of energy of which all his human Aspects are manifested. Biblically stated, Man is thereby "*quickened by the Spirit*", thus effecting a Spiritualization of his entire Beingness.

As a consequence of being quickened by the Spirit of God, meaning that the Light of God has accelerated Man's Beingness into Spiritual Frequencies, causes all of his human Aspects to be Spiritually-enlightened. Since the seven

Aspects of his humanized condition consist of vibratory frequencies in low, earthly, carnal levels, therefore the ultra-high Spiritual Frequencies of Divine Light radiating from his Christ-Center cause his seven-fold Beingness to become Spiritualized and Illumined. The typical human of the world thus becomes super-human as a consequence of experiencing Spiritual Enlightenment...the "*Moksha*" of Hindus, the "*Nirvana*" of Buddhists, the "*Kingdom of God*" of Christians, the "*Secret place of the Most High*" of Jews. Through consistent concentration and meditation upon the Christ-Light within the soul, the words of Jesus then become a personal experience..."*If thine eye be single, thy whole body shall be full of Light*".

In such manner and only in such manner do you attain Oneness with God. For, God is Light, Pure Spiritual Light, and to experience Enlightenment requires that you become fully harmonized and attuned with the Light of God. And since the Light of God is within you -- and correspondingly, "*the Kingdom of God is also within you and not lo here, or lo there*" (to quote Jesus) -- therefore, to achieve Spiritual-enlightenment and the Kingdom of God it is mandatory to attain a state of Oneness with God and His Light, the Christ-Light within your heart.

Through Enlightenment you become a more genuine Expression of God while yet in human form. Through Spiritual Enlightenment you become Spiritually-anointed -- Christed -- and consequently arise from the mass-consciousness of Earth's humanity as a God-Enlightened Prophet or Master. You have, through Enlightenment, overcome and transcended your self-created bondage to this physical-material plane of Life-expression and consequently regained your original Expression of the Creator's Infinite Wisdom, Universal Love, Cosmic Power, Immortal Life and other Attributes.

You have thus re-established and regained your original Oneness with your innate God-Essence. And your Oneness with your God-Essence now permits the Light of God, the Christ-Light at your heart to again radiate throughout your entire Beingness. Initially, the Christ-Light extends from your heart as brilliant Gold, Pink and Blue Radiations which relate to the Creator's primary, principal Attributes of Wisdom, Love and Power. And from these primary colors then radiate the other four colors of the spectrum, thereby causing all seven Spiritual Centers, the chakras, to become activated. Consequently, the Seven Rays permeate your seven-fold Beingness and extend outward as a beautiful aura of glorious colors.

You have thus attained, in your present human embodiment, the Kingdom of God and consequently express on Earth as a God-enlightened, immortal Prophet or Master capable of demonstrating to Earth-bound humanity the Wisdom, Love, Power and other

Attributes of God. Additionally, as a God-enlightened Prophet or Master you will also demonstrate Man's return to his Spiritual Abode through a glorious, rapturous ascension into Realms of Spirit from whence you strayed. Furthermore, you will become the pristine Being of Light, an immortal, infinite Cosmic Being you were created to be from the very beginning of your creation!

* * *

THE SPIRITUAL HIERARCHY
and
THE GREAT WHITE BROTHERHOOD

Chapter 5

God-Consciousness a Requirement

To experience a state of God-enlightenment as a great Saint, Prophet or Master it is mandatory to re-establish and regain your original Spiritual Consciousness. Regaining your original Spiritual Consciousness, regaining your long-dormant God-Consciousness, would harmonize and attune your total Beingness with the Creator's All-Consciousness. This means that your innate Spirit of God would become fully expressive by allowing It to be attuned and harmonized with the Creator's omnipresent Spirit pervading the limitless Omniverse.

Consequently, as a great Prophet or Master, or as an Ascended Being such as a great Archangel, Lord or God, you would be capable of expressing the Creator's Attributes in the form of Transcendent Wisdom, Cosmic Power, Eternal Life and other Attributes. Thus, your original immortality, dominion over the earth and Cosmic Consciousness would again be expressive from your innate God-Self and Its associated God-Consciousness.

As have God-enlightened Beings attained to their innate Godhood, so will you...sooner or later, whether in this human embodiment or another in the future. You have free-will given to you by your Creator and it is for you to decide when your Ultimate Destiny is to be attained. However, the Creator's Love from within your soul can not be resisted. And though you may continue to misdirect your free-will into worldly illusions and procrastinate returning to your True State in Life yet, inevitably, you and all other human souls will be drawn by the irresistible Divine Love of the Creator to their Spiritual Abode from which you and they had strayed.

This Divine Love of the Creator is related as "*the Grace of God*" in some Scriptures, and is an impersonal, universal, dispassionate Love that accepts every human soul as a Son of God. And though as a sinful, prodigal son or daughter, regardless of past sins and transgressions, each soul is lovingly accepted into the Father's House as soon as it turns away from its human and worldly delusions.

The Creator's Love is boundless, it is beyond a human level of love and thus not imaginable or possible for a human. And this Love, augmented by the Creator's Wisdom and Power, will therefore cause you to eventually be raised to the highest possible degree of Godly Perfection in His vast Spiritual Hierarchy of Ascended Beings.

These Beings expressing throughout the limitless Omniverse -- Angelic Beings, Cosmic Beings, God-Beings -- were, at one time, human as you are now. Each of these Ascended Host worked their way up, in consciousness, from a typical human level to a saintly level. From a saintly level they progressed to a semi-enlightened state such as a great Sage (the Sanskrit "*Rishi*") and later becoming as a Spiritualized Adept capable of increasing expressions of the Creator's Attributes and Qualities.

In such manner do the formerly earth-bound humans progress into a more-purified, Spiritualized Consciousness -- a God-Consciousness -- to become as God-enlightened Prophets or Masters...as a Christ, "*the Anointed One*"; as a Buddha, "*the Enlightened One*". Having been God-enlightened they also experience a regeneration, a resurrection, of their entire Beingness and consequently become immortal. For, they have overcome Man's last enemy...death.

In such manner from various past civilizations -- in cloisters, mountain caves, desert retreats or their homes -- such individuals, both men and women, gradually raised and purified themselves from this world's morass of human delusions to become superhuman Prophets and Masters.

Certainly, it is only logical that to experience Spiritual Enlightenment the human consciousness must be changed and transformed from its earthly and worldly quality into a Spiritualized Quality. Saint Paul's admonition "*Be not conformed to the world, but be ye transformed by the renewing of your mind,*"* is an absolute requirement for Spiritual Enlightenment.

* Romans 12:2.

God-Consciousness A Requirement

An enlightened consciousness is a Spiritualized Consciousness, a God-Consciousness, a consciousness that expresses the Kingdom of God. For, the Kingdom of God is a state of Oneness with God, a state whereby the human mind, soul and consciousness expresses God from within itself. The Kingdom of God is not a place somewhere in outer space, but as stated by the God-enlightened, Christed Jesus: "*The Kingdom of God is within you, not lo here, or lo there.*"*

Therefore the Kingdom of God is a state of mind, a state of consciousness. If you realize that the word "Kingdom" is synonymous with the words "*state; realm; domain; dominion*", therefore the Kingdom of God would be the State of God; the Realm of God; the Domain of God; the Dominion of God that is within you.

Therefore when you attain Oneness with God's Presence within your soul, when you attain the state of mind, the state of consciousness of total Oneness with your innate God-Presence, you then express God in and through your human self. You then express and demonstrate the God-Consciousness that all God-enlightened Saints, Prophets and Masters achieved. In this state of consciousness you thus express and demonstrate the Attributes of God...the Wisdom, Love, Power, Life and other God-Attributes as another God-anointed, God-enlightened Saint, Prophet or Master on Earth.

* Luke 17:21.

* * *

THE SPIRITUAL HIERARCHY
and
THE GREAT WHITE BROTHERHOOD

Chapter 6

Experiencing Spiritual Ascension

It is, of course, a definite requirement for all humans to initially become fully enlightened and Spiritualized prior to experiencing an ascension into Realms of Spirit. A human must first become regenerated and resurrected into a God-Consciousness that has been sufficiently purified of a humanized consciousness and thus becoming eligible to be granted a Spiritual Ascension. For, a human must attain a sufficient degree of Spirituality, of being sufficiently Spiritualized, to enter the purity of Spiritual Realms. On entering the Realms of Spirit, such God-enlightened, Christed humans will then become as fully-Spiritualized Beings, as Spirit-Beings, expressing Life and Consciousness eternally in any Realm, Plane or Dimension of the infinite Omniverse.

To repeat, all Ascended Beings had necessarily achieved a FULLY-Spiritualized Condition of their entire Beingness. As a consequence they became as infinite and limitless Spiritual Beings within the Creator's omnipresent, all-pervading Spirit.

It should be realized that a human's total Illumination and Spiritualization causes the mind, soul and body to be merged and blended with the Creator's omnipresent Spirit, thus that human's entire Beingness no longer remains attached to the gravity of Earth. When ascended, when merged and blended with the Creator's omnipresent Spirit, that human's Beingness becomes completely limitless among the many galaxies, universes, stars and planets throughout the infinite Omniverse. The total Spiritualization of that human's Beingness causes it to be completely weightless and beyond the limitations of time and space in this three-dimensional plane of Earth.

Public witnessing and recording of Spiritual Ascensions have been very sparse in scriptural writings, usually due to seclusion of the God-enlightened Saint, Prophet or Master in a monastery, convent, ashram or his own home. Significantly, an ascension occurs only when the individual has FULLY overcome and transcended the human self and this third-dimensional plane of Earth. Thus not many humans have fulfilled this rigid requirement of transcending all that is human and earthly. The Bible and other Holy Writ of the world depict only a few of such individuals who have achieved this Ultimate Goal of human souls.

The God-enlightened, Christed Jesus served as a notable example of a Spiritual Ascension which he demonstrated publically and witnessed by over 500 persons on the outskirts of Jerusalem.* However Elijah's Spiritual Ascension, described biblically as "*a whirlwind into*

* Luke 24:51; Acts 1:9.

heaven", was only witnessed by his disciple, Elisha.* Each of these men to have become worthy and eligible to experience a glorious, rapturous ascension into Realms of Spirit were, of course, required to overcome and transcend ALL that is human and earthly.

A Spiritual Ascension therefore requires an initial God-enlightenment, a regeneration and resurrection from this gross, humanized condition into Oneness, At-Onement, with the individual's innate Presence of God, his God-Self...thus to express God in and through his human self as a Spiritually-enlightened Saint, Prophet or Master. And secondly, that enlightened Saint, Prophet or Master must remain TOTALLY consecrated in Oneness with God until he attains a complete Spiritualization of his Beingness to consequently become as a Being of Light. In such manner he transcends Earth's gravitational forces to enter Realms of Spirit and Light.

The Creator as Pure Spirit is also Pure Light, Pure Crystal-clear Spiritual Light. However, Spiritual Light is not visible to typical human vision because Spiritual Light is beyond the vibratory frequencies of electronic light. And when a human becomes sufficiently Spiritualized into total Oneness with the Creator's Pure Spirit, that human's mind, soul and body is thereby transmuted by the Creator's Spiritual Light residing within the soul. Consequently,

* II Kings 2:11.

such a human, such a fully-transmuted, fully-Spiritualized Individual can ascend from this planet at will and becomes infinite and limitless in the Totality of the Creator's All-Spirit. That Individual has thus returned to his Spiritual Abode to join the Creator's vast Spiritual Hierarchy as an Ascended Master, the Buddhist "*Chohan*".

In such manner have formerly earth-bound humans attained to "*Heaven*"...not through any salvation of personal Saviors or rituals, but only through a personal overcoming and transcending of their human self and this world of Man-made illusions and delusions. The human self and its world-conditioned consciousness must be fully purged, cleansed and purified of its carnal contamination and thereby transformed to a God-infused Consciousness.

To experience a rapturous Spiritual Ascension the human consciousness must become a fully-Spiritualized Consciousness so as to be harmonized and attuned with its innate God-Self and thus with the All-Spirit, All-Consciousness and All-Life of the infinite Creator. In other words, the Creator's infinite Spirit, Consciousness and Light are finally permitted to again radiate within and throughout the human mind, soul and body into a more total Expression of Spirituality and Godhood for that human. That human has thus regained his/her original state of Life and Consciousness as the Creator's pure Image and Likeness!

*   *   *

THE SPIRITUAL HIERARCHY
and
THE GREAT WHITE BROTHERHOOD

Chapter 7

Ascended Masters

When a total Spiritualization and resulting Ascension is attained by a Prophet or Master, that ascended Individual now becomes ONE with the Creator's Infinity after ascending. Now the total human self with its mind, soul and body becomes an infinite Being, a Spirit-Being expressing greater God-Attributes than yet-unascended Prophets and Masters are capable of expressing.

For example, genuine, though yet-unascended, Prophets and Masters have been God-enlightened and thus resurrected into an immortal condition. They are consequently capable of remaining immortal in their human body for many centuries, if deemed necessary. Such God-enlightened Prophets and Masters are also capable of super-human wisdom and power. Comparably however, an Ascended Master, having become as a Spirit-Being, is FULLY Spiritualized (as compared to an unascended Prophet or Master) and thus in purer, more-complete ONENESS with the Creator's All-Spirit, All-Consciousness and Pure Light.

Ascended Masters are therefore capable of expressing greater degrees of the Creator's infinite Wisdom and Power, as compared to yet-unascended Prophets or Masters in physical bodies. Furthermore, Ascended Masters, having become as Spirit-beings, also radiate greater degrees of Spiritual Light and thus described as radiant and beautiful Beings of Light when revealing themselves to worthy humans on Earth.

As an example, a great Ascended Master of antiquity, having ascended thousands of years ago and now expressing his innate Godhood as the Archangel Gabriel, appeared several times to humans on Earth. As a Being of Light he revealed himself to Daniel to teach him of the Truth of his Beingness as a Son of God, thereby causing Daniel to become a God-enlightened Prophet.

Many years later Gabriel also appeared to Joseph and Mary, and then to Zacharias and Elisabeth to inform them of sons to be born to them and to be named as Jesus and John. And about 600 years later, Gabriel appeared to Mohammed and gave him a Spiritual Teaching which became the Qur'an, the Bible for millions of Semitic people now identified as Moslems. As a result of his exalted experience with Gabriel appearing to him as a glorious Being of Light, Mohammed was later God-enlightened as a Prophet of God.

The God-enlightened, Christed Jesus, as an Ascended Master, has also appeared to several worthy humans...notably to Saint Francis of Assisi during the 12th century and also to Pope John XXIII in the early 1960's. Jesus' mother, Mary, has also been appearing as a "*beautiful*

Lady of Light ", usually to pure-minded children. Appearing in Guadalupe, Mexico in 1531, Mary later made apparitions during the 18th century in France, one during 1846 in La Salette to two young girls, and twelve years later in Lourdes, appearing on eighteen separate occasions to a young girl.

Mary's apparitions in Lourdes brought forth the now-famous Grotto and many people to be healed of various illnesses. Later, during 1917, Mary made six successive monthly appearances to three children in Fatima, Portugal, where she prophesied World War II and of cataclysmic conditions to occur at the end of this 20th century if humanity did not turn to God.

Mary, as a great Ascended Master, also fulfills Spiritual Service as an Archangel, for she is the Divine Complement, the Twin Spirit of the Archangel Raphael. Having much love for Earth's humanity, especially for children, she is now being named as "*Mother Mary*" by advanced seekers of God. As a loving mother she has therefore continued to appear in various areas of the world to implore us to turn to God and foretelling of dire conditions if humanity continues its iniquities and warfare.

Recently during a period from June 1961 to November 1965, Mother Mary made dozens of appearances to four girls at Garabandal, Spain. This series included apparitions of Saint Michael, the Archangel, and also of a local priest who had "*died*" seven days before. Then during the 1980's, Mother Mary appeared at a

Coptic church near Cairo, Egypt, and also at a Roman Catholic church in Medjugorje, Yugoslavia. Other apparitions of this Ascended Lady Master are continuing in various areas, however not being publicized by the media or the Vatican. Indeed her deep concern for the pitiful state of Earth's humanity is also evident in the tears flowing from the eyes of her statues in many churches.

Although the above examples of abilities and powers of Ascended Masters exceed those of Prophets and Masters in human bodies, yet Man's Ultimate Destiny is beyond the level of an Ascended Master. The Realms of Spirit are limitless and the Realm of Ascended Masters is but the first level for ascended human souls. For, the ascended state is but an initiatory level, an initiatory Spiritual Station in the Creator's vast Spiritual Hierarchy. The Creator's many Mansions are indeed limitless and many further opportunities await a newly-Ascended Master involving ever-higher, more-perfect Realms, Planes and Dimensions of the infinite Omniverse.

Indeed, when compared to its human expression on Earth, a soul can remain in abject poverty and suffering, or can improve such pitiful conditions. A laborer, for example, can arise from his lowly estate and become a manager or executive of a firm. All human souls have been granted a Divine free-will and are not victims of circumstance, but create their own conditions, their own "*karma*", from embodiment to embodiment to embodiment. Thus a human soul can remain in bondage to this 3-dimensional earthly plane of repetitive birth-to-death experiences, or can become as a limitless, immortal Being in Realms of Spirit.

Eventually, every soul will raise itself from its self-made, death-oriented bondage to Earth and attain its True State in Life. It is but a matter of realizing one's TRUE identity as a Spiritual Being.

Innately, every human is the Spiritual Image and Likeness of the Creator's infinite Spirit and is therefore the INDIVIDUALIZED Expression of the Creator. Consequently, every human Spirit is the SON of God. Therefore, every human soul is potentially a God-Being...but, unfortunately, blinded and captivated by a physical-sensual expression of Life as a physical-material Being on this small planet called "*Earth*".

* * *

THE SPIRITUAL HIERARCHY
and
THE GREAT WHITE BROTHERHOOD

Chapter 8

The Spiritual Hierarchy

Of the 10-billion human souls originally allocated to this planet, the few thousand already ascended are now a part of the Creator's vast Spiritual Hierarchy. These ascended souls from our planet form but a small percentage of millions of Angelic and Cosmic Beings expressing and serving throughout the limitless Omniverse and its many galaxies, universes, stars and planets.

Throughout the many areas of this limitless Omniverse are groups of Beings that are formed and identified as Brotherhoods, Federations and other names. Those Beings associated with our universe of twelve planets and a Sun are identified as Members of the Great White Brotherhood.

Each of these Beings in the Great White Brotherhood aid and minister to all levels of human souls within our universe in an impersonal, universal, dispassionate manner in accord with Cosmic Law, always expressing the Creator's Wisdom, Love and Power. Their Service to humanity includes many types, but emphasizes teaching, guiding and raising all possible souls into their Ultimate Destiny. With selfless Divine Love these Spiritual Beings strive to regain every soul's True State in Life as they did.

Some of these glorious Spiritual Beings achieved their ascension millions of years ago, while others that may or may not be recorded in present-day Scriptures achieved their ascension more recently. As former humans they have returned to their Spiritual Abode from whence they once strayed and now are Members of the Great White Brotherhood and of the vaster Spiritual Hierarchy.

The Spiritual Hierarchy is founded on the Creator's omnipresent Expression, or Beingness...which is, to repeat, Spirit, Consciousness, Light. The Creator's Expression of Beingness as Spirit, Consciousness and Light is basically founded on two primary, principal Attributes... Wisdom and Love. Through the Creator's Expression of Wisdom and Love then causes a third principal Attribute to come forth...Power, Cosmic Power.

Consequently, from a harmonious Expression of Wisdom, Love and Power then extend four additional Attributes, thus resulting in a total of seven Foundational Attributes and Qualities of the Creator.* These seven Foundational Attributes and Qualities of the omnipresent Creator then become the seven-fold Causal Principle and Law of All-Creation and

* For details of the Creator's Beingness of seven Attributes refer to the Aquarian Revelation given this writer by the Creator.

All-Life which governs and manifests all there is throughout the Omniverse. The biblical allegory of Genesis describes this seven-fold Causal Principle and Law of Creation, in a symbolic manner, as merely involving a period of "*seven days*" that the Creator required for creating Planet Earth.

Of course the Spiritual Hierarchy being composed of Spiritual Beings, Beings that have ascended from their humanized condition, each express the Creator's seven Foundational Attributes and Qualities. Each of these Beings having been originally created as the Creator's Image and Likeness are capable of expressing the Attributes and Qualities of the Creator in accord with the degree of Oneness they developed with their innate Divinity, their Spiritual Self, their own God-Self. It was through a consistent love and devotion to their innate God-Self, the Spirit of God within their souls, that these Beings had become Spiritualized from their humanized state and consequently earned their Spiritual Ascension.

Each of the Ascended Beings are therefore capable of expressing and demonstrating the Creator's Attributes and Qualities consisting of Wisdom, Love, Power, Life and others. They are eternal in the Heavens, having eternal expression of Life and having access to any degree of the Creator's Infinite Wisdom, Divine Love and Cosmic Power they wish to bring forth.

However in all expressions of the Creator's

Attributes and Qualities, in all expressions of their innate God-Attributes and God-Qualities, each Ascended Being is enjoined to not ignore or adulterate the Creator's Cosmic Law. For, the Cosmic Law is the Causal Principle of All-Creation and All-Life and therefore the CAUSAL Principle of each Being's expression of Life, Consciousness and Beingness. Consequently any adulteration of the Law, any mis-use of the Law by a Being's egocentric desire for greater Power or self-importance and self-aggrandizement will result in a demotion of that Being within the Hierarchy, even to the extent of becoming de-Spiritualized into a humanized state again.

Therefore the Cosmic Law predominates throughout all of Creation, throughout the limitless Omniverse and its numerous Realms, Planes and Dimensions. The principle of cause and effect in Cosmic Law is in expression everywhere in the Omniverse no differently than in this earthly plane. For, the Law is the Creator's Expression of Beingness and therefore omnipresent and all-pervading as the Creator's sevenfold Causal Principle of All-Life and All-Creation.

Consequently the Law is the very Heart and Essence of every Being's expression of Life and Consciousness, whether as an Ascended Spirit-Being or as an unascended Being in an earthly body. And if an unascended humanized Being on Earth desires to become an Ascended Spirit-Being, it is incumbent upon that yet-humanized

Being to live by and fulfill all requirements of the Creator's Cosmic Law. For, admittance into the Spiritual Hierarchy is founded on COMPLETE compliance with the Law and, in fact, any Spiritualization of humanized Beings is utterly impossible until ALL requirements of the Law are fulfilled.

The Spiritual Hierarchy and each of its many Brotherhoods and Branches throughout the Omniverse is therefore composed of Spirit-Beings that are in complete, total harmony and compliance with Cosmic Law. They are pure and pristine Beings that are totally humble and selfless in their service for the Creator and His Will, regardless of possible sacrifices to their expression of Life and Beingness. In accord with their degree of humility and selflessness, in accord with their quality of service in compliance with the Creator's Will, they are then granted and blessed with increasing expressions of the Creator's Attributes of Wisdom, Love, Power and other Attributes.

In accord with the Law and its principle of cause and effect each Spirit-Being is consequently graded commensurate with his/her personal loyalty and accomplishments within the Hierarchy, or degraded if not fulfilling his/her service within the Hierarchy. Thus the entire Hierarchy and each of its various Brotherhoods and Branches all function as One Spiritual Unit, each Being serving the Whole in total selflessness and love for the benefit of the entire Omniverse and all its physical and material creations, whether planetary, human or elemental.

THE SPIRITUAL HIERARCHY
and
THE GREAT WHITE BROTHERHOOD

Chapter 9

You Are The Son Of God

Of course, as the Image and Likeness of his Creator, Man is "*the Temple of God*"*, he is an inseparable part of the Creator's seven Foundational Attributes and Qualities. Also, Man was necessarily created as a part of, as an aspect, as a distinct, Individualized Expression of the seven-fold Causal Principle and Law of Creation. Thus, Man's Beingness is inseparable from the Creator's seven-fold Causal Principle and Law of Creation. This means that Man's expression of Beingness, his expression of Consciousness and Life, is a direct, integral part of his Creator's omnipresent Consciousness and Its seven Attributes.**

For example, the Creator's three principal Attributes of Wisdom, Love and Power are expressed in and by Man, except at an adulterated human level: as thought/intelligence, emotion/ feeling and energy/strength. Additionally, Man's entire Beingness is inseparably integrated with his Creator's seven Octaves and Planes of Creation whereby his human, earthly expression is composed of seven aspects. These

* I Cor. 3:16; II Cor. 6:16. ** For details of the Creator's Beingness of seven Attributes refer to the Aquarian Revelation given this writer by the Creator.

seven aspects of Man's Beingness are: Spirit, mind, soul, mental body, emotional body, astral body and physical body. Moreover, Man's innate Christ-Consciousness or Christ-Self, is composed of seven Spiritual Centers...the Sanskrit "*Chakras*", symbolized in the Bible as "*seven candlesticks*" and "*seven lamps*".*

Since Man's expression of Life, Consciousness and Beingness is inseparable from the Creator's seven Foundational Attributes, it is only logical that the Creator's Spiritual Hierarchy is also founded on and expresses these seven Attributes. For, the Hierarchy is composed of former humans who consummated their Spiritual Ascension and thus expressing the Creator's Attributes...except at higher, Spiritual Levels. The Hierarchy of Spirit-Beings therefore expresses greater and purer degrees of the Creator's Pure Spirit than yet-unascended, unenlightened human souls.

The Creator's Pure Spirit, His All-Consciousness, is therefore expressed as seven Foundational Attributes and the seven-fold Creative Principle and Law of the Omniverse. Furthermore, Pure Spirit is Spiritual Light, therefore the Light is also divided into seven Qualities, into seven Octaves or Rays of Light comparable to refraction of the Sun's electronic light into the color spectrum or "*rainbow*" of

* Chakras: Sanskrit, meaning "wheels". Described in the Bible as "seven lamps" & "seven candlesticks" (Exodus 25:31-37; Revelation 1:12-13.).

seven colors.

Furthermore, since the Creator's Beingness as Spiritual Light is also the All-Consciousness, the Supreme Consciousness permeating the Omniverse, therefore the seven Octaves or Rays of Spiritual Light are actually seven REALMS of Consciousness permeating the limitless Omniverse. As a consequence, these seven Octaves or Rays of Spiritual Light and their associated Realms of Consciousness form the foundational Expression of the Spiritual Hierarchy and its functions throughout the many galaxies, universes, stars and planets of the Omniverse.

Within our universe of a Sun and twelve planets that part of the Hierarchy, identified as the Great White Brotherhood, is thus responsible for creating, manifesting, energizing and governing these twelve planets and all thereon. Although Earth's humanity believes that the God, or Allah, or Brahman, or Jehovah to Whom they pray is the actual and only Creator of all there is, it must be realized that the Creator is, essentially, Pure Spirit, Pure Crystal-clear Light, Pure Consciousness.

It must be deeply realized that the Pure Spirit, the Spiritual Light, the Pure Spiritual Consciousness of the Creator is ever-pristine and perfect, never adulterated or weakened into any lower vibratory frequencies such as electromagnetic energies or psychic energies which compose the visible and invisible forms of Creation. It is thus a profound Truth that the Creator is always Ultimate Perfection and never of any lesser quality. The Pure Spirit and Pure Consciousness of the Creator is never intermixed, involved in, nor adulterated with any lower expression of Consciousness as expressed by human souls, but constantly remains as Pure Crystal-clear Light.

Since the Creator's All-Consciousness is constantly in the highest possible frequency of Spiritual Light, therefore all creations and manifestations below His Realm of Pure Spiritual Light are brought forth by His Individualized Expressions, His Image and Likeness. This means that all which is of lower vibratory frequency than Spiritual Light, all which is composed of energies -- whether of a physical, material or psychic nature -- is manifested by Ascended Beings or, when of a lower nature, by humans. Consequently, within our universe of a Sun and twelve planets it is the Hierarchy, identified locally as the Great White Brotherhood, that is responsible for creating, manifesting, energizing and governing the planets and all thereon.

However, it must be realized that all of the Creator's Individualized Expressions of Life and Consciousness, whether Ascended Spirit-Beings or humans, are not actually true Creators, but only co-creators. For example, a "*miracle*" brought forth by a Spiritual Master is not an authentic or true creation, but only a manifestation, only a materialization of something produced from the surrounding energy, or atoms.

Chapter 9

In reality, only energies should be recognized as an actual creation, for they are a lower order of Spirit. Energies originally came forth from Spirit as a slower frequency of vibration. Any physical or material thing, being composed of solidified energies, is therefore not an authentic creation because it is composed of a lower vibratory frequency than either Spirit or energy and thus not a true creation, but only a materialization, a manifestation of energy.

Spirit is the basic, primary Essence of All-Creation, the Creative Principle and Power in which and from which all Beings, all energies, all forces, all manifestations are in expression. Only because of Spirit, as the Creative Principle and Law of the infinite Omniverse, can any form of creation or manifestation be possible.

Furthermore, Spirit is the foundational Cause and Principle of all Life and Consciousness expressing everywhere, whether throughout humanity or every form of Nature. Whether the energies, or humanity, or forms of Nature, all are an expression of the Creator's omnipresent Spirit and Beingness radiating as and founded on seven Foundational Attributes.

Therefore the Life and Consciousness expressed by Spirit-Beings and earthly humans is dependent upon our Creator's omnipresent Spirit and Beingness composed of seven Foundational Attributes. Neither Spirit-Beings or humans are some type of autonomous entities expressing Life and Consciousness in an independent manner...but are an integral, inseparable part of the Creator's Cosmic Ocean of Spirit, just as you are now inseparably immersed in Earth's atmosphere.

Consequently whether Ascended Beings or unascended human souls, each express Beingness only because they are Expressions of the Creator's all-pervading Beingness. It is only because of the Creator's immanent and all-encompassing Spirit that any form of Life and Consciousness -- whether Spirit-Beings, humans or elementals -- can live, and move, and have their Beingness.

To reiterate, the Creator is Pure Spirit, Pure Consciousness, Pure Light filling the limitless Omniverse. The Creator is not, as erroneously believed by some religious sects, an anthropomorphic Being, nor any type of Divine Person or Personality residing on some distant planet or sitting on a throne somewhere in space.

As Pure Spirit, Pure Consciousness, Pure Light permeating the Omniverse, the infinite Creator therefore needs Individualized Expressions of His omnipresent Beingness. In other words, Individualized Beings are required to express the Creator's ever-Pure Consciousness at lower levels and to thereby manifest things below His Realm of Pure Spirit and Light. Consequently, the Creator's only Son is His Individualized Expression of Beingness, His Image and Likeness. Whether an Ascended Being or unascended Man, this is the Creator's Son, His Individualized Progeny having all His

Chapter 9

Spiritual Attributes.

Therefore you are the Son of God. Your true identity and potential is clearly stated by St. John and the Master Jesus: "*Beloved, now are we the Sons of God, and it doth not yet appear what we shall be...*"; "*The Father loveth the Son and hath given all things into his hand. He that believeth on the Son hath everlasting Life, and he that believeth not the Son shall not see Life...*"*

Since the Creator's Consciousness is constantly in the highest possible purity and vibratory frequency of Spiritual Light, all creations and manifestations below the Realm of Spiritual Light are therefore brought forth by His Sons, His Individualized Expressions of Consciousness and Life. This means that all which is energy, all which is composed of various energies, all which is of a physical, material or psychic nature is manifested by Ascended Beings and, to a limited degree in this world, by humans, by you.

* I John 3:2 & John 4:35-36.

* * *

THE SPIRITUAL HIERARCHY
and
THE GREAT WHITE BROTHERHOOD

Chapter 10

The Great White Brotherhood

As previously stated, the Ascended Beings functioning in our universe as a Branch of the Creator's vast Spiritual Hierarchy are identified as the Great White Brotherhood. This Brotherhood is initially founded upon the Creator's Cosmic Law. And since the Cosmic Law is an integral part of the seven-fold Creative Principle, the Great White Brotherhood is also an integral part of the seven-fold Creative Principle. Moreover, the Great White Brotherhood is a Spiritual Expression of the Creator's seven Foundational Attributes.

This Great White Brotherhood, this Spiritual Brotherhood within our universe of a Sun and twelve planets is composed of hundreds of glorious Ascended Beings, thousands of Angels, and a number of God-enlightened Prophets and Masters who express in physical bodies on some of these planets. The primary structure of this Brotherhood, the basis on which it is primarily organized, may be compared to the organizational structure of a large business firm in which there is a Board of Directors and necessary executives such as a president, various vice-presidents and other administrative personnel who manage that firm, its employees and its functions.

Chapter 10

The initial or topmost function of this Administrative Branch of the Great White Brotherhood serving our universe would, of course, first require an application of the Creator's PRIMARY, PRINCIPAL Attributes... that is, to first bring forth the Creator's active Expression of Wisdom, Love and Power into our universe. In this regard, it must be clearly understood that these primary, principal Attributes do not function, nor other Attributes of the Creator express in an activated, dynamic manner throughout the entire Omniverse. The Creator's Attributes are not fully expressive throughout all "*interstellar space*", except in certain localities in which are galaxies and their component universes, stars and planets.

Though the Creator is omnipresent and fills all space throughout the Omniverse, however in vast spaces BETWEEN galaxies the Creator's Attributes are in a rather dormant, passive, non-expressive Condition. As Pure Spirit and Consciousness occupying the limitless Omniverse, the Creator therefore needs Individualized Expressions of His Beingness in order to express His Attributes in specifically designated areas of the Omniverse. For, to repeat, it is only from and through His Individualized Expressions of Life and Consciousness, His Image and Likeness in the form of Spirit-Beings, that the infinite Spirit and Consciousness of the Creator becomes fully expressive and creative.

In our universe it is therefore through the Great White Brotherhood that the seven-fold

Creative Principle becomes activated and dynamic. This is initially begun from expression of the Creator's three primary, principal Attributes of Wisdom, Love and Power. For, to repeat, these three Attributes of the Creator are the basis and foundation for any and all types of Creation, or any and all expressions of Life and Consciousness. These three Attributes of Wisdom, Love and Power are therefore the PRIMAL TRINITY of the Creator, the primary, foundational Principle of the Creator's Expression of Consciousness and Beingness.

Of course, these primary Attributes of the Creator -- the Wisdom, Love and Power -- are also expressed in His Image and Likeness, in both Ascended Beings and unascended humans. However these Divine Attributes occur in varying degrees of expression among both Ascended Beings and unascended humans only IN ACCORD with their Spiritual Attunement with the Creator.

In humans, as previously stated, these Divine Attributes are adulterated, filtered and weakened whereby the Creator's Wisdom is expressed as mere thought and intelligence, the Love as typical human emotion and feeling, the Power as only physical strength and energy. In comparison, among Ascended Beings and among God-enlightened Prophets and Masters in physical bodies the degree of Wisdom, Love and Power that is expressed is of a purer quality. However, in each case, whether Ascended Beings or Prophets and Masters on

Earth, the degree of their personal ability to express these Divine Attributes is always commensurate with their degree and quality of Spirituality...their degree of Purity and Oneness with the Creator's Pure Consciousness and Light.

It is therefore important to understand that the degree of Purity and Oneness with the Creator's Consciousness and Light is dependent on the degree of IMPURITY, the lack of maya*, in a human's consciousness. Though a human consciousness was originally a pure, undefiled Angelic Consciousness, originally a Spiritual Consciousness expressing as the Creator's Image and Likeness, however after its separation from Realms of Spirit the Angelic Consciousness became humanized. Consequently this humanized consciousness became increasingly enamored and attached to physical and material things of Earth and thereby contaminating the inherent Purity of the Creator's Consciousness and Light within itself.

Such contamination of the Creator's Consciousness and Light, resulting from thoughts and feelings, of psychic attachment, to physical and material things thus caused the maya, the psychic veil of illusion, to become as a thickening layer of "*psychic soot*" enveloping the mind, soul and consciousness. Through the principle of cause and effect in Cosmic Law the

* "Maya"; Sanskrit, meaning "illusion; that which is of creation; temporal and transitory manifestations."

earth-bound, humanized consciousness was building-up increasing degrees of such psychic soot as negative karma* for itself. And due to continuing interests and attachments to physical and material things during successive human embodiments, caused the layers of psychic illusions, the psychic soot, to delude and mislead the mind, soul and consciousness farther from the Creator's Purity of His Consciousness and Light.

Thus each fallen Angelic Being, having become seriously earth-bound and contaminated with much negative karma, must retrace his/her steps from this "*far country*" and "*wilderness*" of the world. Originally coming from the Divine Source, each humanized Angelic Being must eventually return to that Source. For, until the original Oneness with the Divine Source is attained, the humanized Being can only remain in the outer darkness of an illusory, self-caused world separated from the Infinite Wisdom, Universal Love, Cosmic Power, Immortal Life and other Attributes of the Creator. The humanized Being thus remains limited in expressing the Creator's Attributes which are inherent within that humanized consciousness. That humanized mind, soul and consciousness will therefore continue in its human limitations and problems resulting from ignorance, carnality and repetitive physical deaths.

* "Karma"; Sanskrit, meaning "effect; product; result." Thus consequences of Cosmic Law as cause & effect.

Chapter 10

It is therefore a definite requirement for every human on Earth -- if a return to his/her Divine Source is desired -- to mitigate, to dissolve the accumulations of maya, the psychic illusions and delusions manifested during this and past embodiments. The Spiritual Purity of the original Angelic Being must be regained if Oneness with the Creator is desired. A Spiritual Ascension to the Divine Source of All-Life, All-Consciousness and All-Beingness is not possible through any doctrine, creed, dogma or ritual conceived by humans nor through any martyrdom of a Prophet or Master to "*forgive the sins of sinners*" or "*dying as their Savior*". Spiritual Ascensions of humans are only possible when the self-created human self is dissolved to its original nothingness. Only when the human self is totally surrendered to the Spiritual Purity of the innate, long-dormant Angelic Being is a Spiritual Ascension possible.

Therefore the accumulated dross and contamination within the human consciousness, the negative karma -- the maya, the omissions and commissions not in accord with the Creator's Law -- must be cleansed and purged from the human consciousness before becoming eligible for a Spiritual Ascension. The Law decrees that a human's negative karma, the sins, iniquities, omissions and commissions in opposition to Cosmic Law, must be LESS than the positive karma of "*good works*" committed in compliance with the Law. Thus only when the good, positive karma reaches at least 51% of the human consciousness, when the negative karma is reduced to no more than 49%, only then is the human eligible to be accepted into Realms of Spirit.

To become an Ascended Being in the Great White Brotherhood of our universe therefore requires a relatively purified consciousness. Certainly a typical human consciousness of this world, a consciousness not harmonized with its own God-Presence, a consciousness yet contaminated with much worldliness and carnality, a consciousness that must yet become Spiritualized as a God-enlightened Saint, Prophet or Master, is not ready to enter the Realms of Pure Spirit. Such a consciousness would not be of any value to the Creator nor to the Brotherhood, but a contaminant and a problem that yet requires purifying and maturing to express its inherent Presence of God and a Christ-like God-Consciousness.

*   *   *

THE SPIRITUAL HIERARCHY
and
THE GREAT WHITE BROTHERHOOD

Chapter 11

Creation Of Our Universe

Regarding the creation of our universe, or solar system, the Creator's three primary, principal Attributes are initially brought into Expression by two glorious Beings of Light. These Beings are actually great Lords, named Helios and Vesta, who radiate the Wisdom and Love from within the Sun. By first expressing Divine Wisdom and Universal Love in a balanced, harmonious manner, these two Lords then bring forth the third Attribute of Power. As a consequence these three Attributes become activated and dynamic throughout this area of the Omniverse which is to become as our universe, or solar system.

Then commencing from these three primary, principal Attributes radiate the remaining four Attributes, which completes the seven Foundational Attributes, the seven Octaves or Rays that compose the Creator's Totality of Consciousness. This causes the seven-fold Cosmic Law and Creative Principle to now become fully dynamic and operative for creating anything needed by Ascended Beings or humans. From the Heart of the Sun these two Lords of Light therefore bring forth all Attributes and Qualities of God into Expression for creating, manifesting or energizing any needs within this area of the

Omniverse.

From this point, the Power-Attribute can now be put into active, dynamic Expression to bring forth the creation of planets. For, the Cosmic Law and associated Creative Principle of seven Octaves or Rays can now be applied. This is accomplished by the Seven Spirits of Creation, as these glorious Beings are usually called. They are titled in Hebrew as "*Elohim*".

Consequently, with the Power-Attribute now usable in co-ordination with the other Attributes, these Seven Spirits of Creation apply and activate this Cosmic Power to cause various energies to come forth and become dynamic. And with and from the resulting energies these Seven Spirits then manifest and materialize the planets by causing a stepping-down, a slowing-down of vibratory frequency of the component atoms and electrons.

The Seven Spirits of Creation, the seven Elohim, that presently express in our sector of the Omniverse -- including both male and female counterparts -- are named: Apollo and Lumina; Arcturus and Victoria; Cyclopea and Virginia; Hercules and Amazonia; Heros and Amora; Peace and Aloha; Purity and Astrea.

Thereafter, the final stage in the creation of our universe, involving the aspect called "*Nature*" on the planets composing our universe, was accomplished by seven Archangels. These seven Archangels each express in one of the seven Octaves or Rays as do the Seven Spirits of Creation and also include both male and female counterparts. These Archangels serve to manifest various types of Life and Consciousness throughout our universe...that is, they have brought forth and manifested the many types of Life-forms and different aspects of Nature upon the planets.

Since that original manifestation of Life-forms and aspects of Nature, these seven Archangels have continued to manage and maintain these manifestations. Additionally, they have other responsibilities associated with their great Spiritual Authority...such as also teaching and guiding human souls. These seven Archangels therefore stand at the head of the seven Rays of Life and Consciousness within our universe. This means that they continue to radiate these seven Rays so as to maintain, energize and nourish all forms and expressions of Life throughout our universe...including human, elemental and angelic.

The seven Archangels that presently express in our sector of the Omniverse -- including male and female counterparts -- are named: Chamuel and Charity; Gabriel and Hope; Jophiel and Christine; Michael and Faith; Raphael and Mother Mary; Uriel and Aurora; Zadkiel and Amethyst.

Then, in addition to the seven Archangels, there are seven Ascended Masters who also have important responsibilities and great Spiritual Authority in the next level of the Brotherhood's Administrative Branch. Each of these Ascended Masters also express and serve in one of the seven Rays and associated Attributes of the Creator. These seven Ascended Masters, to complement the seven Archangels, then govern, guide, supervise and teach these expressions of Life and Consciousness on the planets... especially that of humanity, whether incarnate or discarnate. Serving in the Brotherhood's Administrative Branch, each of these Ascended Masters also have Legions of Angels to aid them in governing, guiding or teaching these various expressions of Life and Consciousness throughout our universe of twelve planets.

This entire universe is consequently manifested, sustained and governed in a state of Divine Order, Harmony, Wisdom and Love in accord with the Creator's Will and Cosmic Law. As a Spiritual Brotherhood founded on Cosmic Wisdom and Divine Love, all Beings express as ONE, each expressing as an impersonal, selfless, inseparable Consciousness within the Creator's omnipresent Supreme Consciousness. All Spirit-Beings, whether great Lords, Archangels, Masters or lower Orders of Angels, each aid and serve the Brotherhood in a selfless manner. Moreover, each of these Beings also serve -- in a selfless manner -- the billions of human souls and every aspect of planetary manifestations... each in accord with their individual aptitudes and development of personal Attunement with the Creator's Attributes.

Furthermore, through wise management from the Administrative Branch of this Great White Brotherhood, each of the twelve planets are maintained and governed in their orderly, precise orbits around the Sun...meaning that members of the Administrative Branch and their Legions of Angels are not only responsible for bringing forth the Creator's Cosmic Power but also for maintaining the resulting energies. Their maintenance and application of the energies further includes a precise regulation for the orbits of many satellites, the "*moons*", around planets. Additionally, the required energies throughout each planet and all aspects of Nature are also sustained and governed in a continuous manner by these great Spiritual Beings and the many Angels, Devas and Nature-Spirits that are involved in all of this Creation.

* * *

THE SPIRITUAL HIERARCHY
and
THE GREAT WHITE BROTHERHOOD

Chapter 12

Your Ascension Awaits

In addition to the seven Elohim, seven Archangels and seven Ascended Masters in the Administrative Branch of the Great White Brotherhood, there are many other great Masters and Lords in other Branches of the Brotherhood busily serving, manifesting and maintaining planetary requirements throughout our universe. But regardless of their Branch of Service, each is primarily engaged in the progression of human souls. For, whether incarnate or discarnate, all souls are always a priority and must be aided in expanding their consciousness so that as many as possible are brought into a Spiritualized Consciousness and Oneness with their innate God-Self.

As these great Ascended Beings have themselves experienced, such Spiritualized souls would thereby experience their resurrection, their regeneration from an earth-bound, humanized condition to cause a subsequent ascension into Realms of Spirit. As a result to return to their Spiritual Abode from whence they strayed and thus to progress in accord with their Creator's Cosmic Plan into Ultimate Perfection.

For, such newly-Spiritualized and ascended human souls -- as Ascended Masters -- will then gradually replace the seven Masters (Sanskrit:

"*Chohans*") presently in the Administrative Branch of the Great White Brotherhood. Later, they will have opportunities to progress into other and higher Stations of the Brotherhood involving greater Divine Wisdom, Cosmic Power and Spiritual Authority. And thereafter, if desired, they can continue to progress within the Creator's vast Spiritual Hierarchy in other areas of the limitless Omniverse, into different universes and, later, even other galaxies.

The opportunities and potentials awaiting all human souls are, indeed, unending in the Creator's many Realms, Dimensions and Planes of Life and Consciousness. The Creator's Cosmic Plan is to bring every worthy soul into increasing Perfection. For, His Will is for all human souls to attain their True State of Life-expression as glorious, immortal Celestial Beings. The Creator has never decreed human souls to experience gross, earthly embodiments, nor any suffering and death.

Our Creator's ONLY Will for His prodigal Sons and Daughters is that we return to our Father's House from whence we had strayed. All human souls reap what they sow, they cause their own karmic consequences in accord with the Cosmic Law which they ignore and flaunt. To seek and to strive for any egocentric, self-centered human goal or "*worldly success*" only leads to eventual self-destruction...death. Conversely as admonished by Jesus: "*Seek ye first the Kingdom of God and His Righteousness (right-useness of His Law), and all things shall* *be added unto you."**

One of the Creator's primary, principal Attributes is Love. But this Love is not the typical human type of love, the human feelings and emotions involving sentiments, sympathies, sensual and sexual passions, the weekly "*fellowshipping*" of typical churchianity and other examples of human expressions of love. These are not of a pure Spiritual Quality but only of a mental and emotional nature, only of the human mind, soul and senses.

As stated biblically, "*God is no respector of persons.*" Therefore, the Love that God the Creator IS, is a Love that is completely dispassionate, impersonal and universal, a Love that is purely Spiritual. This clearly indicates that God is not involved with nor attached to any thing or to any human, but in a constant state of Pure Spirit and Light. Thus, though humanity continues having warfare, or experiencing plagues, famines and various problems, God does not interfere nor extend sympathy toward such conditions, nor are Ascended Beings permitted to do so.

The Will of God is that His Progeny, His Individualized Expressions of Spirit, overcome and transcend their self-caused, humanized condition and return to their Spiritual Abode from whence they once departed. The Will of God and the Love of God are not involved with the human personality, the persona, nor its

* Matthew 6:33.

mis-creations, but only to the innate Divinity, to the Spirit-Part, to the God-Part that God created, while the human part, the personality is what the human ego created.

Man is composed of seven aspects. The four lowest or carnal aspects are those termed as his four lower bodies...the physical, the astral (or etheric), the mental, and the emotional bodies. Each of these are a product of Man's present earthly embodiment, thus a product of Earth. The physical body is composed of Earth's energies, of atoms, in a coalesced, solidified form. The astral body is also composed of Earth's energies in an etheric form. The mental body is composed of psychic energies resulting from thoughts, ideas, beliefs, etc. expressed by the individual. And the emotional body is composed of psychic energies resulting from emotions, feelings, desires, lusts, etc. expressed by the individual.

These four lower bodies of Man, as products of an earthly embodiment, are but temporal, transitory aspects of Man's expression of Life and Consciousness as a Spiritual Being. It is these four earthly aspects of Man's Beingness that must be overcome and transcended from their earthly, carnal state into a purified, Spiritualized State.

As stated biblically: "*For, this corruptible must put on incorruption, and this mortal must put on immortality. So, when this corruptible shall have put on incorruption, and this mortal shall put on immortality, then shall be brought* *to pass the saying that is written,* DEATH *is swallowed up in victory!*"*

Significantly, it is only as a result of God's Love that Man can ever overcome Earth. The Love of God is the greatest Quality of God, but the most misunderstood. The Love of God is a purging/purifying Power. This purging/purifying Power of God's Love causes self-discipline. God's Love disciplines the adult and the child. God's Love disciplines the four lower bodies of Man that have deviated from His Law. If God expressed typical human emotions and feelings toward children as do many permissive parents and teachers, if human egos were forgiven their misdeeds and iniquities, if spared from experiencing negative effects and pain after transgressing the Law, humans wouldn't have any learning opportunities from their misdeeds. As wise Solomon stated, "*Spare the rod, and spoil the child.*"**

Regardless of "*modern*" theories to not restrict the free expression of children, nor of adults, to "*do their own thing*", the Law of God requires that the human, carnal part of Man must be overcome and transcended if his Ultimate Destiny in Life as an Ascended Being is to be consummated. However, modern "*psychological*" theories disregard and ignore the fact that Man's Ultimate Destiny in Life involves walking on the proverbial "*razor's edge*".

* I Corinthians 15:53-54.

** Proverbs 13:24; 22:15; 23:13; 29:15.

Chapter 12

Regardless of this fact, professional religionists, leaders of religion, usually insist that "*many paths lead to God*"...attempting to convince possible converts that their form of religion is the only true path to God. However a genuine Teacher stated very clearly that there is only ONE WAY leading to God, only ONE PATH that leads through a straight and narrow gate: "*Enter ye at the strait gate, for wide is the gate and broad is the way that leadeth to destruction -- and many there be which go in thereat -- because strait is the gate and narrow is the way which leadeth unto Life, and few there be that find it.*"*

Unquestionably, since Man was created as the Spiritual Image and Likeness of God and since the Kingdom, or State, of God is within Man and not lo here or lo there, therefore it is only logical that the ONLY path to God is directly to His Presence within Man. And to attain this Kingdom or State of God, to attain Oneness of God's Presence within the human self, apparently requires a subjection, a submittal, a surrender of the human self to its Presence of God. For, it might be asked, "*How else can the outer human self become harmonized with its innate God-Presence, its God-Self, if not blended with its own God-Self? How can the human self become God-enlightened and Spiritualized if not surrendering itself to its God-Self, if not merging and blending the entire human self --*

* Matthew 7:13-14.

body, mind, soul and ego -- into and with its innate God-Self?"

Only when, and only when, a complete merging and blending of the human self with its innate God-Self is attained, only then can the God-Self express Its God-Attributes in and through the human self. Only then can the human self express immortal Life and Consciousness on Earth as a God-enlightened Prophet and Master. And only then can that human self express and demonstrate its inherent and long-dormant Attributes of God...the Wisdom, Love, Power Life and others as a genuine, full-fledged Prophet or Master. For, only after the human self has surrendered, merged and blended itself with the innate God-Self can it be possible to become "*the anointed*", to be Spiritually-anointed as another Christ, Buddha, Mother Mary, Elijah, Ezekiel, Krishna, Zarathustra and many other God-anointed Prophets and Masters throughout human history.

It is therefore mandatory that the human self -- the self-created earthly manifestation in opposition to the Law and Will of God -- is submitted and surrendered to its own God-Self if a Spiritual Ascension is desired. Unfortunately, however, such surrender of the human self does not occur instantly, but only until it becomes sufficiently humbled and selfless through many difficulties, problems and sufferings. Thus the Love of God, balanced with His Wisdom, causes the human self to

ter 12

Law and Will. After
s and negative karma
odiments, the human
lly comes to its senses --
ill, Father, but Thine
decides to return to the
ence it came.
r, only through complete
ler of the human self to
e earthly human be born
f Spirit from whence he/
Again complying with
e human self experiences
ough sincere dedication
on God's Presence with-
ngdom and State of God
fulfilling Jesus' admoni-
single, thy whole body
',* the human self thus
s Spiritual Enlightenment
l by God to become a
nscious Prophet or Master.

Consequently, such a God-illumined, God-conscious Prophet or Master serves and expresses the Great White Brotherhood on Earth as a Spiritual Teacher, a true Guru. In this capacity as a Spiritual Teacher, as a God-conscious Prophet or Master, pure Spiritual Teachings are offered to Earth's humanity, Divine Teachings and Revelations

* Matthew 6:22.

brought forth directly from God or from various Ascended Beings in the Brotherhood. As a consequence that increasing numbers of humans become God-enlightened and thereby returned to their Spiritual Abode and the Kingdom of God they left behind.

In such manner do humans regain their Spiritual Heritage, to again conjoin their consciousness with the Creator's All-Consciousness. The Creator's All-Consciousness is within the human soul as the Kingdom and State of God, and the only requirement is for the entire human self -- the body, mind, soul and ego -- to be conjoined in total Oneness with that All-Consciousness and Kingdom of God within itself. Consequently, the Love of God, in only seeking Divine Perfection for the human, brings forth and causes a glorious and rapturous Spiritual Ascension for that human. The human becomes totally Spiritualized and ascends from Earth as a glorious Angelic Being. The Spiritualized human thus arises from Earth *"...to meet the Lord in the air..."**

Consequently, the former humanized Being becomes an Ascended Being, an Ascended Master, who has overcome the human self and the world. As an Ascended Master, he/she now becomes a full-fledged member of the Great White Brotherhood and the vaster Spiritual Hierarchy composed of uncountable Spiritual Beings that inhabit the many galaxies, universes, stars and planets throughout the limitless Omniverse.

* I Thessalonians 4:17.

*   *   *

THE SPIRITUAL HIERARCHY
and
THE GREAT WHITE BROTHERHOOD

Chapter 13

This World a Miscreation

Clearly, this world, this civilization is but a Man-made thing, a fantasy and illusion of Spirit-Beings that became enthralled and deluded with a physical-material expression of Life. This world, this civilization was not a creation of God-centered Beings in the Great White Brotherhood and certainly not in accord with the Creator's Cosmic Plan. This world is but a manifestation of Earth's humanity, a miscreation of fallen Spirit-Beings in opposition and defiance of the Creator's Will and Law. This Man-made world is therefore in a constant state of division, chaos and violence. In fact, this world is an abomination to the Creator.

If Mankind on this planet now suffers from increasing droughts, violent storms, torrential rains, earthquakes, floods, volcanic eruptions, pestilences, famines and other so-called "*acts of God*", it should now become general knowledge that any and all climatic or geologic disturbances are basically due to human iniquities.

Any imbalance of Nature's Forces, any cataclysmic disruptions of Earth's terrain are not due to the Creator's "*vengeance*" upon humanity nor "*punishment for sins*". It is only logical that Mankind's many evils and contamination of Earth's ecology, Mankind's continuous interference of our planet's Divine Harmony and "*Balance of Nature*" causes much climatic and geologic turbulence from their natural vibratory frequencies that is completely unnatural. Sinking of both the Atlantean and Lemurian continents, plus a tipping of Earth's axis which caused the "*ice ages*" are but three cataclysms of the past resulting from Mankind's many iniquities.*

Although the Great White Brotherhood continues to reharmonize Earth's energies, Mankind continues to disrupt them with senseless nuclear explosions or constant barbaric warfare in some part of this world each and every day. In addition, though unknown to most scientists, humanity's insane crimes and violence, its many hatreds, bigotries and greeds, its billions of thoughts, feelings and emotions of a negative, evil nature have been emanating psychic energies that are further disturbing the electromagnetic (atomic) energies of which Planet Earth is composed.

Shamefully, not only is Earth's atmosphere, its surface structure and its rivers, lakes and oceans greatly contaminated with nuclear radiations, industrial wastes, and various pesticides and chemicals, but its surrounding psychic plane is also seriously contaminated. For, Earth's psychic plane is now permeated with humanity's negative, evil psychic energies -- the

* Refer to Aquarian Revelation, by this author, for specific facts and details of these and other cataclysms.

"*brain-waves*" of science and "*thought-forms*" of metaphysics -- that are causing the ever-increasing turbulence throughout this planet.

It should not require a scientific genius to understand that human thoughts and feelings emanated as an energy, a psychic energy, will affect Earth's terrain and atmosphere. For, all manifestations are composed of energies. Therefore, the negative, evil nature of most psychic energies emanated by human minds and souls cause much disharmony and turbulence throughout Earth's terrain and its enveloping atmosphere and ionosphere. It is thus apparent that unless a drastic change occurs in humanity's mass-consciousness, ever-greater climatic and geologic crises will manifest.

Meanwhile, this universe of twelve planets and a Sun, this galaxy with its many stars and other universes, plus the limitless Omniverse of many other galaxies, universes, stars and planets, each continue to function in Divine Order and Harmony in accord with the Creator's Cosmic Law. Furthermore, in accord with the Creator's Plan, all Creation, every galaxy, universe, star and planet, every aspect of Nature will continue to evolve and progress into ever-increasing Divine Perfection in accord with His Wisdom and Love.

However, this Race of Man on Earth is generally unpredictable, yet immature, not even cognizant of his innate Divinity nor of the Cosmic Law. Apparently due to erroneous, contradictory religious doctrines and materialistic academic curricula, the mass-consciousness of Earth's humanity is in a state of ignorance regarding the Truth of their very Beingness in relation to their Creator's Law and its principles of Life and Creation.

Significantly, this planet was intended to be as a school-room for human souls to evolve and bring forth their innate Divinity into expression. It was therefore created with a beautiful terrain to provide an attractive, pleasant environment for humanity, thus causing the Brotherhood to describe this planet as "*the Green Emerald*". But this Race has not progressed as it should have to this time of Earth's transition into a new Cosmic Age. Consequently, at this transitional period of Earth into the Age of Aquarius and a New Cycle of Life-expression, humanity has become increasingly turbulent as vibratory frequencies approach ever-higher Spiritual levels.

Foreseeing the increase of such human turbulence with related violence and warfare, the Creator, through the Brotherhood, has been taking preventive action to mitigate any self-destruction of Earth's humanity as occurred in past civilizations. Therefore to prevent another planetary cataclysm from possible use of nuclear energy by power-mad politicians and militarists to control the world, and/or a great increase of negative psychic energies to further disturb Earth's balance of Nature, various advanced Teachings have been offered to re-direct human consciousness into Spiritual Reality. These Teachings are of different levels to attract all possible humans into an expansion of consciousness from their orthodox, materialistic or atheistic thinking into Cosmic, Spiritual levels.

As Earth's transition into a New Cosmic Cycle involving the prophesied new heaven and new earth progresses, a "*channeling*" of many Teachings from advanced Beings in the astral plane have thus been awakening many progressive and liberal thinkers into an awareness of other planes of Life. Additionally, through dictations from Ascended Beings in the Brotherhood and Spiritual Hierarchy, or through Spiritual Communions directly from the Creator, profound Teachings, Prophecies and Revelations have been offered to expand human consciousness into a Spiritually-enlightened God-Consciousness.

An example of one profound Spiritual Teaching, a recent Discourse from the Ascended Master known as the Christed Jesus, is herewith offered. Received by a dedicated seeker of God and Light-bearer, this Discourse is quite factual about world conditions and offers important prophecy and guidance for humanity into the New Age and New Cycle on Earth, the biblically-prophesied new heaven and new earth:

"*Greetings, beloved Light-bearers of Planet Earth! It is I, 'The Man of Galilee', 'The Nazarene', he who became known as 'Jesus the Christ'.*

"*In a time of great peril upon Planet Earth, I send this message forth via the hand of one of my Messengers. Yes, I said one, for there are many now stationed on Planet Earth who go forth in my Name. May that which they speak forth prove to be in Harmony and Unity, for this will distinguish the true speaker of Truth from those who speak according to their own interpretation thereof. Harmony/Unity... keep this foremost in mind!*

"Shortly shall the words of the prophecy be fulfilled: 'Two women shall be grinding at the mill; one shall be taken and the other left'. Dost thou wonder at those words? Allow me to explain: None shall enter through the narrow gate lest the Laws of the Cosmos are adhered to. Think not to ride the Road to Glory due to the fruits of somebody else's labors. Nay! I say, it shall not be!

"Rumblings of war and agitation of various sorts are heard ringing through the ethers surrounding Planet Earth. It shall be up to the inhabitants thereof to decide whether 'war' or 'peace' shall be the motto of the day! Yes, you have two opposing forces presently at work, and the outcome shall be far-reaching as to whether it be the Forces of Darkness, or the Forces of Light who emerge from the battle as victors.

"Not much longer shall the turmoil be allowed to prevail upon this planet. All the Cosmos is in readiness, and I tell you truly, Earth shall claim her rightful place in my Father's House of many Mansion-worlds. Those who steadfastly oppose her transition shall be dealt with according to their own actions, and shall be recipients of suitable 'rewards'!

Chapter 13

"As I said long ago to those who then walked the dusty roads of a far-away land with me: 'I go to prepare a place, that where I AM ye may be also'. I have prepared such a place. In fact, more than one place has been prepared, so there shall be room for all... regardless of the manner in which they choose to exercise the gift of free-will. I must assure though, that none who seek to destroy this 'Green Emerald' planet shall remain thereon, for they shall be removed therefrom and placed elsewhere, in a place more suitable.

"It is well to understnd that this beautiful planet, that we of the Spiritual Planes call the Green Emerald, has been created to serve as a 'school-room' for its human inhabitants. Each of you have been in this earthly school-room during many physical embodiments...yes, throughout many Cosmic Ages and even Cosmic Cycles of Earth-time. You have had many learning-experiences and grades should not have to be repeated if sufficient wisdom has been gained to graduate into a Spiritual Consciousness.

"And now in this time of Earth's transition into a New Age and a New Cycle, I speak of 'Graduation-time' for some of you. And I tell you it is at hand! See that ye are well-prepared...for, as it has been stated in your Bible, there shall be no 'repeaters' this time. Earth shall know a new type of humanity during the upcoming New Age.

"Soon shall the Song of Freedom be sung by all of those who have been in bondage and servitude to those who have tried to divert Planet Earth from her True Course and Divine

Birthright. Make no mistake about that! And Planet Earth shall claim that which is hers, according to the Plan of her Creator!

"Itchy fingers are presently at the 'switch' which can trigger a global holocaust. Heed this warning and be aware! Preparation is, indeed, called for, and I tell you truly...your best preparation, Light-bearers of Planet Earth, is to put on the full Armor of Light. And, stand ye therein! Let your Light so shine that others shall be guided to you. For, there in your Light many who would otherwise travel the wide road leading in various directions may, instead, seek the narrow path which leads to safety.

"I have been called 'The Light of the World'. And, so shall each and every Light-bearer of Planet Earth also be known as a "Guiding Light'. For, you shall go forth in my Name, illuminating the way for those who still seek a way out of Earth's present dilemma.

"I shall stand beside you, Light-bearers, for I know my own. Go ye forth in Unity of Purpose, and let thy Light shine!

*"I AM Jesus, 'The Light of the World', also known to Planet Earth as a "Babe in Bethlehem'; 'the Man of Galilee'; as 'the Christ', as 'the Son of God'."**

* This Discourse from Jesus received by a Messenger named Joyce Hodge Davis.

* * *

Chapter 14

The Holy Trinity

Of course, all humans, as the Creator's Individualized Expression of His Life and Consciousness, as His Spiritual Image and Likeness, are therefore destined to progress into Divine Perfection to a greater degree than any other aspect of Creation. In fact, these Individualized Expressions of the Creator's Spirit and Conciousness are destined to reach a MORE-EXPANSIVE degree and quality of Divine Perfection than any other aspect of Creation. For, when human souls are adequately Spiritualized and experience their Spiritual Ascension, then -- as Ascended Masters -- they will replace the seven Masters presently belonging to the Administrative Branch of the Great White Brotherhood.

Such new Masters within the Brotherhood's Administrative Branch, if fulfilling their service in accord with the Creator's Will and Plan, will then be granted a great degree of Divine Wisdom and Power. Later, they will have opportunities to progress into higher Stations of the Brotherhood that involve greater degrees of Spiritual Authority, God-Wisdom and Cosmic Power. And thereafter they will have added opportunities to enter the Creator's vast Spiritual Hierarchy throughout other areas of the limitless Omniverse, into different universes, and later even other galaxies. Indeed, you, as your Creator's Image and Likeness, do you realize "*All that the Father hath, is thine?*"

The Creator's Love is boundless. Truly, His Cosmic Plan and Will for every human soul and each Ascended Being is to achieve a Spiritual Progression into ever-increasing Divine Perfection. As a consequence, so that all of His Individualized Expressions of Consciousness and Life, all the billions of His sons and daughters will become as His co-Creators throughout the limitless Omniverse.

This indicates a mandatory requirement for a human soul...that the Trinity specified by Jesus -- Father, Son and Holy Spirit -- must be attained on a PERSONAL basis. For, this is a secondary and personal Trinity which applies to Man's Spiritual Sonship, your Sonship, with the Creator. This secondary Trinity stipulates that when preceded with water baptism -- symbolically meaning a cleansing and purification of the human consciousness -- that the Creator's Sons should bring forth their original relationship with their Father. This original relationship, of course, is only possible through a Holiness or Wholeness of the Sons' human consciousness and Spirit with the Father's omnipresent Spirit.

Thus, the Father and the Son would become inseparable as One Whole Spirit, or Holy Spirit. Such a human then becomes Spiritualized and God-enlightened as a TRUE Son of God. Or, stated differently, since Spirit is Consciousness, attaining the Holy Spirit or Wholeness of Spirit results in a HOLY Consciousness, a WHOLE Consciousness of total Oneness with the Creator's Supreme All-Consciousness...as compared with a typical human consciousness separated from the Creator's All-Consciousness. The human consciousness is consequently transmuted into a God-Consciousness and can then truly exclaim, as did Jesus, "*I and my Father are ONE!*"

In such manner does a fallen Spiritual Being, a Being originally created as the Creator's Spiritual Image, a pristine Angelic Being that has degenerated into an earthly humanized condition, regain his/her original state of Divinity. The earth-bound humanized Being becomes de-humanized and re-Spiritualized to his/her original God-Consciousness as an Ascended Master. Having regained the original God-consciousness and ascended into Realms of Spirit from whence he/she once became separated, a complete liberation from three-dimensional, physical-material attachments and interests has been achieved.

However, even an Ascended Master within the Brotherhood, when providing Spiritual Teachings to yet-humanized Beings, can become excessively involved with some humans in a personal manner. Though God-Consciousness and Oneness with the Creator has been achieved, yet an emotional, sentimental interest and attachment can develop between that Master and some human on Earth. A newly-Ascended Master is especially vulnerable to such attachments, since, in most cases, 49% of his/her negative karma must yet be transmuted while fulfilling various aspects of Spiritual Service. And some subconscious memory-patterns and ties to certain members of Earth or to an individual of the opposite sex can still remain in that Master's consciousness.

Though yet a Novitiate in the Brotherhood, but if the newly-Ascended Master remains steadfastly dedicated to the Creator and fulfills all facets of Spiritual Service in a satisfactory manner, the negative karma yet remaining is gradually transmuted from the consciousness and a promotion into a higher Station of the Brotherhood is then offered. The Novitiate Master has overcome certain testings and initiations required by the Creator's Law and therefore worthy to be trusted to enter a more important level of Spiritual Service within the Brotherhood. As with ordinary humans, unearned Spiritual Powers are not offered indiscriminately, nor any laws and principles for precipitating material things permitted the human until becoming sufficiently dependable and mature to be trusted with such Powers. A child can not be trusted with matches because of not comprehending their fire-power, nor is a Novitiate in the Brotherhood offered any use of tremendous Cosmic Powers that are yet beyond his/her comprehension.

The entire Brotherhood and Hierarchy is

therefore governed by the Creator's Law whereby every Being is constantly tested to be completely worthy and dependable before any promotion into a higher Plane of Life and Consciousness can be earned. For, each higher Plane within the Hierarchy offers ever-greater expression of the Creator's Wisdom and Love and thus ever-greater degrees of His Cosmic Power. Each Being, whether a Novitiate Master or a great Cosmic Being, therefore progresses within the Hierarchy in accord with the degree and quality of Wisdom and Love that is expressed. As previously stated, it is upon the Creator's primary, principal Attributes of Wisdom and Love that form the basis of His Beingness and upon which His Law and Will are founded. It is upon this basis that Cosmic Power and all forms of energy are produced. And from the three primary Attributes of Wisdom, Love and Power the Attribute of Life, the Life-Force, and other Attributes are then radiated throughout the Omniverse.

It is therefore in accord with the degree and quality of Wisdom and Love that each Spiritual Being progresses into higher Levels and Stations of the Hierarchy. As expressions of Wisdom and Love -- in a BALANCED MANNER -- are improved and expanded, then greater degrees of attunement and oneness with the Creator's Infinite Wisdom and Perfect Love are achieved. Thus ever-higher Levels and Stations in the Hierarchy are earned with greater degrees of Spiritual Authority and Cosmic Power granted that Being. In these Levels and Stations of the Hierarchy, which are ever-higher and purer Realms and Dimensions of Spirit, that Being experiences ever-more-perfect and glorious expressions of Life and Consciousness. For, in the Creator's All-Consciousness, in the Father's House are many Mansions...indeed, many Mansions without limit throughout the infinite Omniverse.

In such manner a fallen Spiritual Being returns into Realms of Spirit from whence he/she strayed and degenerated into a humanized Being. The humanized Being, by simply reversing the process, by living in accord with the Creator's Law and Will, is regenerated into a Spiritualized Being. By simply expressing ever-higher degrees of wisdom and love in every-day thoughts and feelings, the humanized consciousness becomes increasingly Spiritualized.

Indeed, no limitations exist for any human to attain the very highest level and quality of Life and Consciousness in the Hierarchy, for the Life and Consciousness that every human expresses is the Creator's Life and Consciousness expressing within the human.

It is therefore incumbent, only sensible, for a human to live a TRUE religion, a religion that leads the human directly to the Creator's Presence, to the God-Presence, the Father within the soul. Only by living a TRUE religion is it possible to attain the Holy Trinity involving the Father, Son and Holy Spirit. Only when the human attains Union and Oneness with the

Father as His original Image and Likeness, then the human is again Spiritualized.

Consequently the human regains his/her Wholeness with the Father and becomes Whole with the Father, no longer separated and divided from the Father. Having dissolved the dualism between the Father and the Son -- between the Father and His Image and Likeness -- the Son attains to Monism and Wholeness with the Father. And in this state of Wholeness, or Holiness, the Son becomes Holy, becomes a Holy Trinity with the Father. The Father and the Son thus become as One Whole Spirit!

* * *

THE SPIRITUAL HIERARCHY
and
THE GREAT WHITE BROTHERHOOD

Chapter 15

Becoming God-Enlightened

To become God-enlightened requires attainment of God-Consciousness, a Consciousness of Oneness with the Creator's Beingness within you. If, however, you still express a humanized consciousness, a consciousness yet having worldly interests and involvements, a consciousness yet having attachments to other humans and material possessions, then practice of TRUE religion is mandatory. For, TRUE religion and God-Consciousness requires a CONSCIOUS and CONSTANT consciousness of Oneness with God in all daily interests and activities, otherwise a total God-enlightenment will yet be delayed. It must be realized that each and every interest and activity involves various thoughts and feelings, and if an interest or activity is of a worldly and earthly nature, of but a mundane physical-material nature, the consciousness is then programmed with the related thoughts and feelings.

Therefore practice of TRUE religion is absolutely IMPERATIVE if you desire God-enlightenment and God-Consciousness. For, when God-enlightened into a conscious Oneness with God you become as an immortal Prophet or Master. The true and original meaning of religion must consequently be applied and lived to achieve your Ultimate Destiny in this human plane of Life.

The original meaning of "*religion*" from the Latin "*religio*" is: "*to unite; to bind back; to bind together*". Similarly, the original meaning of "*yoga*" from the Sanskrit root-word "*yuj*" is: "*to hold fast; to bind together; yoke*". Thus when you unite, bind back, bind together your human self with God's Presence within your soul, then your total Beingness -- mind, soul and body -- becomes God-enlightened. Simultaneously, your Beingness is also re-united, merged and blended with the All-Spirit and All-Consciousness of the omnipresent, all-pervading, immanent Creator of ALL THERE IS.

Since the Creator's Spirit and Consciousness is not only omnipresent around you but also immanent within you, therefore His Beingness is actually the Source and Essence of your entire Beingness. In Truth, you could not BE in existence, you could not express any Life, Consciousness or Beingness if the Creator would withdraw His Spirit and Consciousness from this planet. Therefore, the Creator is actually expressing His Beingness in you, with you, and through you. You are truly expressing your Creator as "*the Temple of God*"...but, unfortunately, subjugating and blocking a full Expression of His Beingness and Attributes with your present humanized consciousness.

Frankly, do you not recognize your self, think your self, feel your self, see your self as a human personality, as a human-Being, instead of a Spirit-Being? Therefore, it becomes mandatory -- if desiring God-Consciousness and consequent resurrection -- that you begin to recognize your human self as merely composed of earthly matter and energy. It is not of Pure Spirit. And this recognition must also include the world...which probably involves most of your interests, thoughts and emotions each day.

Your human self and this world only composed of earthly matter and energy are therefore not a permanent Reality nor in accord with your Creator's Will. The ONLY Reality and in full accord with the Creator's Will is His Nature. The Creator's Nature is Pure Spirit. Consequently, the ONLY Reality, that which is permanent and eternal is SPIRIT, all else is but temporal illusion subject to continuous change, decay, disintegration and death.

Truly, "*The Kingdom of God is within you; not lo here, or lo there*".* Therefore realize that the word "*Kingdom*" is synonymous with the words "*state; realm; domain; dominion*". Consequently the Kingdom, State, Realm, Domain of God is within you. And when you attain this Kingdom or State of God, when you attain to the State of God-Consciousness whereby the Father and you the Son become as One Whole Undivided Spirit, you then are God-enlightened and regenerated. You are then regenerated and resurrected to that original

* Luke 17:21.

expression of Life and Consciousness that you had before your separation from the Father... from your innate God-Self and God-Consciousness.

In that original State of God-Consciousness you would also express a "*dominion over the earth,*"* that original God-Dominion you had before becoming deluded with carnal and sense-bound earthly interests. You would again express your God-Power over energy and matter as is possible for God-enlightened Prophets and Masters and, of course, expressed by all Ascended Beings.

This leads you to the conclusion that applying Wisdom and Love related to and toward your Creator -- which is, actually, to your own God-Essence -- is the ONLY way to attain your Ultimate Destiny. You can therefore realize that expressing thoughts, feelings, emotions, interests which only relate to Spiritual Reality and no longer to human, worldly illusions would increasingly transform your conscousness into higher vibratory frequencies.

Indeed, applying a simple psychological principle of expressing loftier Spiritually-oriented thoughts and emotions each and every day will transmute and raise the quality of your consciousness to become increasingly expressive in Spiritual Frequencies of Cosmic Wisdom and Divine Love. And as you express increasing degrees of the Creator's primary, principal

* Genesis 1:26-28.

Attributes, then the third principal Attribute of Power becomes possible for you. Through transmutation of your consciousness from a human level to a Godly Level you thus begin to express as a superhuman Prophet or Master!

However, as a word of warning when achieving this exalted state of God-Consciousness, it is mandatory that the love for your God-Essence remains dedicated and consistent. Tragically, certain humans throughout Mankind's history, after attaining Spiritual Enlightenment and God-Consciousness, became self-centered and egocentric, they began to center a love upon their human self rather than their God-Self. As a result, the God-Power from within their Being became overshadowed, subdued and subjugated by their contaminated consciousness resulting from selfish, negative desires.

The Creator's Cosmic Law can not be circumvented nor evaded. Through the principle of cause and effect, even God-enlightened Prophets and Masters, if misusing their innate God-Power for selfish reasons will soon lose that Power. Many Prophets, Masters, Yogis, Swamis, Lamas and even Ascended Beings had their Powers withdrawn from them due to selfish, egocentric desires. For example, Jesus of Nazareth was tempted with a desire for world-power when levitating onto a mountaintop. But he resisted any further temptation with the words, "*Get thee behind me, Satan...*"*

In addition to losing their God-Power such

* Luke 4:5-8.

egocentric Beings also lost their Divine Wisdom. Because their love was not in harmony with the Creator's Universal Love, their Divine Wisdom became adulterated into mere human "*intelligence*". Becoming self-centered, egocentric "*show-offs*", by mis-using the Creator's Cosmic Power as mere sorcerers, magicians or charlatans, such misguided individuals lost their attunement with their own innate Divinity, their God-Self. Also, such loss of attunement with their God-Self deprived them of the immortality, the resurrected condition that was gained from their Spiritual Enlightenment. Furthermore, their egocentric mis-creations in opposition to Cosmic Law caused serious karmic consequences in future embodiments for themselves.

Having the potential of expressing all Divine Attributes of your infinite Creator, it is incumbent for you -- and certainly of greatest benefit -- to ONLY apply and direct your thoughts and emotions, to express your psychic powers ONLY toward achieving your True State in Life. For, you are a Spiritual Being, a God-Being, and therefore an alien on this little planet. Tragically, due to misleading educational and religious standards in this world, most humans mis-use their psychic powers, their mental-emotional expressions, to manifest various problems, privations, illnesses and eventual self-destruction. Yet, it is every human's personal responsibility -- yes, duty! -- to not ignore the very Source and Essence of their Life, Consciousness and Beingness. For, sooner or later, in this embodiment or another, every human soul will have to overcome and transcend this Man-made world of illusions and also Man's last enemy...death.

So, be about your Father's Business and become what you are in Reality. Innately as the Spiritual Image and Likeness of your infinite Creator, therefore God-Enlightenment, resurrection and ascension into Realms of Spirit is awaiting you. Upon your Spiritual Ascension you will, initially, become an Ascended Master. Thereafter, your opportunities are indeed unlimited to attain increasing Divine Perfection in ever-higher and more-glorious Realms, Dimensions and Planes of Life and Consciousness. In addition, you will be granted ever-greater Spiritual Authority and Cosmic Powers as a co-Creator with your infinite Creator throughout the limitless Omniverse!

To quote the Creator:

"It is simply a matter of Spiritual Progression into increasing Divine Perfection, so that as many as possible (of human souls) will eventually become as great Gods. Yes, as great Gods who will be responsible for large galaxies and systems of planets throughout My infinite Omniverse. For, there is much space, so-called, that is yet unoccupied or unused. And much space is yet available, We might say, for many galaxies and universes...and yes, millions of planets and stars.

"So, the opportunities that are available

*and awaiting human souls are, indeed, unending and will lead into ever-more-glorious, more-perfect Levels, Qualities and Expressions of Life and Consciousness in My many Mansions of Spirit and Light. For, My Cosmic Plan of increasing Perfection is to bring forth every worthy human soul to become as a glorious Being of Light...yes, to eventually express as an infinite God expressing all of My Attributes and Qualities as completely as possible throughout My limitless Omniverse!"**

* * *

THE SPIRITUAL HIERARCHY
and
THE GREAT WHITE BROTHERHOOD

Sequel

The facts and principles in this book are basically as offered this author in various Communions with my Creator during past years and as stated in the Communion which follows this sequel.

It is emphasized that, to quote a great Master Teacher, "*Of my self, I can do nothing. It is the Father within that doeth the works.*"* And so it was with this book and my Communion, my Communication, with the Father to obtain actual facts regarding the Original Creation and of the Spiritual Hierarchy and Great White Brotherhood.

Unfortunately, mainstream religion does not believe nor accept that direct Revelation is possible in today's civilization, that the days of God-inspired Prophets have ended with the advent of the Judaic-Christian Bible, the Moslem Qur'an, the Hindu Bhagavad Gita, or other Holy Writ of today's world. However, such reasoning may be but a subtle excuse by today's authorities of religion for their personal failure to attain sufficient attunement with God. Or, is it yet believed, as propagated several years ago, that "*God is dead*"?

I repeatedly stated and emphasized in this book that Man is God's Spiritual Image and

* St. John 5:30; 14:12.

Likeness. All Holy Writ of the world states this foundational truth of Man's Beingness. The very Heart and Essence of Man's Beingness, his expression of Life, Consciousness and Beingness, is God...for, how can Man BE or EXPRESS what and who he is if God is not in expression within Man's soul? Therefore if an individual realizes this fact of his Beingness and -- through deep meditation -- attains a conscious Communication, a personal Communion with his innate Presence of God, then how can authorities of religion refute or denounce such a truly Divine Teaching?

World Religions Not Truly Spiritual

It must become general knowledge, particularly at this period of Earth's transition into a New Age, that any form of religion not of a revelatory quality, if not of direct Revelation for today's humanity, should be regarded as only a conception of Man's finite beliefs and reasonings. The many religions and their often contradictory and competitive sects, denominations and cults are evidence of finite beliefs and reasonings of various humans.

Unfortunately, today's many religions, Occidental and Oriental, are predominantly founded on ancient Teachings and/or Revelations mainly written in very ancient or completely dead languages. In most instances these ancient Teachings or Revelations were originally written by a Spiritual Teacher's disciples and/or students not having the understanding of the Teacher or Guru, thus misinterpreting his Teaching. Thereafter, copies or translations of their writings into other languages were made by various individuals -- self-appointed authorities, priests, scribes, theologians, translators -- who, having even less understanding of mystical, Spiritual Principles within the Teachings, made additional errors in their interpretations and translations.

It must therefore be realized that, in the main, the present-day religions and their many sects, denominations and cults -- regarded as "*mainstream religion*" encompassing both the fundamental and orthodox variety -- are generally misleading. Not founded on direct and pure Revelation, but mainly on various types of doctrines, creeds, dogmas, rituals and even hallowed traditions conceived by self-successive, self-proclaimed authorities over the centuries, therefore today's religions are not of pure Spirit.

Not founded on pure Spiritual Teachings or Revelations direct from God and Realms of Spirit, today's religions are therefore misleading as only superstitious beliefs or, at best, only temporary sedatives for seekers of God. Not as pure Spiritual Teachings, but as shallow doctrines, creeds and beliefs of unenlightened authorities, the mainstream religions and even metaphysical philosophies are incapable of bringing forth a complete Spiritual Enlightenment and God-Consciousness of human souls.

Sequel

Communion With God Mandatory

Spiritual Enlightenment and God-Consciousness initially requires only Communions with God within Man's soul.

If, for example, popular religious doctrines were capable of bringing forth a true Communion from a person's innate Presence of God, such a person would then be offered a pure Spiritual Teaching. Through a pure Spiritual Teaching directly from God, instead of a diluted and misleading "*religious*" teaching based on some sectarian doctrine, creed or dogma, the person's consciousness would become redirected from human and world illusions into Spiritual Reality. The human consciousness would be expanded and transformed from this three-dimensional earthly plane into the Spiritual Planes of Life and Consciousness. Through such expansion and transformation the former humanized consciousness would become a God-enlightened, Spiritualized Consciousness.

It might therefore be asked, "*How can a human consciousness become Spiritualized, how can it experience Oneness with its innate Presence of God, if not becoming capable of some form of harmony and attunement with its God-Presence?*" Certainly if the human consciousness is indoctrinated with a false Man-made religion, if offered only the outer husks of Spiritual Truth merely composed of church-approved, canonized theology, that human consciousness can only remain in the level and quality of that religion. To become Spiritualized, to attain Oneness with God, a human consciousness must necessarily be instructed and directed into a Spiritualized, God-conscious state through proper teaching founded ONLY on Spiritual Truth and, simultaneously, to be PURIFIED of its worldly and carnal contamination.

Entering The Spiritual Hierarchy

It is therefore only with a purified and Spiritualized consciousness that a human can attain Oneness with his/her innate God-Presence to experience the Kingdom of God, Nirvana, the Secret Place of the Most High and thus become worthy of a Spiritual Ascension. As a result of a Spiritual Ascension that human consciousness, that human mind, soul and ego, then becomes a member of the Creator's vast Spiritual Hierarchy of innumerable Ascended Beings inhabiting the limitless Omniverse. For, the Hierarchy inhabits and serves the Creator within the millions of stars and planets throughout the Omniverse and is composed of many groups called Federations, Brotherhoods and other names.

But since humans from this planet called Earth are most familiar with its civilization, with its religions, its philosophies, life-styles, etc., therefore after ascending into Realms of Spirit they will remain in this universe to serve its humanity. In fact, Cosmic Law requires them to serve Earth and its humanity since the Novitiate Master's remaining karma (of 49% or less) must be atoned-for and expiated where most omissions and commissions against the Law were committed. These Novitiate Masters will consequently become members of the Great White Brotherhood that serves this universe composed of Earth and its sister planets.

Your Function In The Brotherhood

The newly-ascended Novitiate Masters, as members of the Great White Brotherhood, will initially fulfill the type and level of Spiritual Service best suited for them. Therefore their Service will generally be in accord with their basic abilities which were developed during their human embodiments. Perhaps some may serve as Spiritual Teachers or Guides for humans, or for discarnate souls. However, others may be better qualified to serve the Brotherhood based on their aptitudes and abilities relating to technical, scientific, artistic or other qualities developed during their tenure as humans. Thus the Brotherhood is relatively self-dependent, functioning in accord with the Creator's Law and Will, but without interference from the Creator in regard to decisions or details for which the Administrative Branch and other senior Members of the Brotherhood are responsible.

It must be realized that the Creator is PURE

Spirit and PURE Light. Therefore the the Creator is PURE Spirit and PURE Light. Consequently the Creator does not become involved in any aspects or details of Cosmic Creation... that is, regarding physical and material manifestations. All physical and material manifestations are the responsibility of His Spiritual Image and Likeness, whether ascended or unascended. The Creator's primary, basic interest is His Spiritual Image and Likeness, His Spiritual Progeny, and not in any creations or mis-creations that humanized or Spiritualized Beings may manifest. It is through His Law and its principle of cause and effect that each Being, humanized or Spiritualized, learns lessons to become ever-wiser and more perfect. Consequently all teaching and guiding of human souls throughout this universe of twelve planets, as well as all planetary requirements, all energies, all manifestations, all aspects of Nature, are the responsibility of Ascended Beings with the aid of thousands of Angels, Devas and Elementals (usually called "*Nature Spirits*" involving the Gnomes, Salamanders, Sylphs and Undines).

Each newly-Ascended Master therefore begins as a novice in his/her field of Spiritual Service and to gradually be raised and promoted to a more expanded Service, a higher Spiritual Station within the Brotherhood. In accord with his/her degree of dedication, selflessness and love a corresponding promotion is offered into a higher, more important Spiritual Station.

As a consequence of earning promotions, a

newly-Ascended Master has the opportunity -- as his/her Spiritual Heritage granted by the Creator -- to express Life and Consciousness in ever-higher, ever-more glorious Stations within the Great White Brotherhood or anywhere else in the vast Spiritual Hierarchy. Every newly-Ascended Master can become a greater Master, or as an Archangel, or as a great Lord, or even as a God or Goddess. Thus every human soul, through a personal free-will, can arise to become as a co-Creator with the infinite Creator, or can continue to remain as a mis-creator, a mis-user of the omnipresent energies in accord with selfish, carnal desires.

True Religion Based On Cosmic Truth

In such manner do human souls -- through expansion of consciousness into Spiritual Reality -- progress into a total Oneness with the infinite Nature and Perfection of their Creator (if that is possible). And in such manner, in accord with the contents of this book, can worldly religions become unified from their many divisions and purged of their inconsistent, contradictory doctrines, creeds, dogmas, rituals, hallowed traditions and other false gods.

At this critical period of planetary transition into a new Cosmic Age, the Age of Aquarius, it is mandatory that humanity is liberated from its lack of Spiritual Truth. The New Age will involve a new world, a new civilization, the biblically-prophesied "*new heaven and new earth.*" Humans must therefore become knowledgeable of their true Beingness as infinite and immortal Spiritual Beings and no longer as but evolved apes. They must become aware of their potential to experience God-enlightenment from their own God-Presence and not remain stifled by orthodox limitations nor misled by shallow scientific theories. And they must be informed that God-enlightenment and associated Spiritualization of their physical body with consequent resurrection from death is possible in their present human embodiment.

Perhaps the facts offered this author in the following Communion from the Creator relating to the Spiritual Hierarchy and Great White Brotherhood will cause an upheaval and renovation of all worldly religions. Indeed to not merely cause a unification and harmony among all sects, denominations and cults of worldly religions into a GENUINE ECUMENISM, but to raise and expand humanity's mass-consciousness into a Spiritualized, God-like Quality. Consequently that the original meaning of "*religion*" from the Latin "*religio*" -- to bind together; to bind back -- and also the original meaning of "*Yoga*" from the Sanskrit root-word "*yuj*" -- to hold fast; to bind together; yoke -- can be fulfilled. Thus that worldly, institutionalized religions and their many sects, denominations and cults will bind back human souls to their original state of Life and Consciousness in Realms of Spirit from whence they strayed.

*　*　*

THE SPIRITUAL HIERARCHY
and
THE GREAT WHITE BROTHERHOOD

The Communion

In conclusion I now offer my Communion from the Creator, exactly as offered me, resulting from my prayerful request for clarification regarding the foundational structure and activities of the Great White Brotherhood and its relationship to the Spiritual Hierarchy:

"A good afternoon to you, My beloved son! Thank you for joining Me in this Communion, a Communion that you have requested. And it is in regard to a question so as to clarify for you the Hierarchy that is active and functioning in your universe. Yes, that part of the Spiritual Hierarchy that identifies Itself as the Great White Brotherhood. And you wish a clarification regarding the structure, the foundation and Its functions.

"So, My beloved son, since this is an important subject and so that you may be correct in your writings or lessons, We will make this as a Discourse-Lesson for you and possibly for others.

"Therefore, in regard to this Great White Brotherhood as a part of My vast Spiritual Hierarchy, let Us initially recognize that It, of course, functions and is founded upon My Cosmic Law. And, as you know, My Cosmic Law is founded upon and an integral part of My Attributes...upon My seven basic and principal Attributes.

"Consequently, this Brotherhood is founded upon and functions in accord with My Law and as an integral part of My seven basic, principal Attributes. And in regard to Its structure, as to the way It is organized, It is basically organized, We might say, similar to the organizational structure of a large business firm in your world, whereby there is a Board of Directors and various principal Officers such as a president and various vice-presidents and certain administrative personnel that function and cause that organization or firm to be successful...whereby they administrate the various employees and control its functions or business.

"And this is quite similar to the Great White Brotherhood of your universe, which is an integral part of My vast Spiritual Hierarchy that functions throughout the limitless Omniverse of many galaxies, universes, stars and planets. And the topmost function of this Great White Brotherhood would, of course, involve My primary, principal Attributes. In other words, to initially bring forth the Expression of My three primary, principal Attributes which, as you know, are Wisdom, Love and Power.

"Please recognize that these Attributes do not function or express in a dynamic manner throughout the Omniverse; that is, throughout what is termed in your world as "interstellar space", except in certain localities in which are galaxies and their component universes, stars and planets. Elsewhere, between the galaxies, My three primary, principal Attributes are, shall We say, in a dormant, non-expressive Condition.

"Thus, in regard to the universe in which you express Life and Consciousness -- and in which this Great White Brotherhood is active -- it is initially necessary that these three primary Attributes are brought into Expression... meaning the Wisdom, Love and Power. And this is initiated by two great Beings on, or shall We say, in your Sun.

"These two great Beings, who are actually great Lords, begin to express the Wisdom and the Love. And, as you know, when in conjunction and harmony, these two Attributes then bring forth the third Attribute of Power. So, consequently, these three Attributes become activated and dynamic throughout your universe of twelve planets. And thereby the Power Aspect or Attribute is put into Expression, into dynamic Expression by the Seven Spirits of Creation, as they are usually called.

"And these Spirits of Creation consequently cause the actual creating, they initiate the creating through the Power-Attribute that has been activated by the two great Lords in the Sun. Consequently, the Power-Aspect has now been activated and made dynamic; whereby the energies are coming forth and being expressed from My Power-Attribute.

"And then, at this point, there are the seven Archangels. And what they serve to do is to bring forth various Expressions of Life and Consciousness into the universe and its planets. In other words, they cause the manifestation of the various aspects of Creation throughout the universe...yes, the various forms of Life and and various aspects of what you term as

"Nature".

"Thus, in different words, the planets are originally created by the Seven Spirits of Creation who bring forth the dynamic Expression of Cosmic Power and also create the planets. And thereafter, the seven Archangels -- whom you know by name -- who bring forth that which is necessary to cause an Expression of Life and Consciousness onto the planets.

"And from that point, then there are the seven Ascended Masters. They, in turn, then control, govern and guide all these aspects of Creation on these planets...especially that of humanity. Of course, they have Legions of Angels who aid them in the controlling, governing and guiding of these various aspects of Life and Consciousness. And, in turn, the seven Archangels also aid in this Service in regard to what these Ascended Masters are involved in.

"And from that point, My beloved son, all of Creation existing on your twelve planets has been created, and governed, and guided by this Administrative Branch of the Great White Brotherhood in your universe. Of course, there are various other Ascended Masters, yes, and Lords who also have great responsibilities and Spiritual Authority in regard to various Branches or Aspects in your universe.

"And, consequently, all throughout the twelve planets of your universe, all is in order, all in harmony. As, for example, the energies are governed and controlled by this Administrative Branch of the Great White Brotherhood, whereby the planets orbit in

in orderly procession and remain in their orbits, and including the satellites around the planets which are called as "moons". And, of course, every aspect of so-called Nature is also controlled and governed through this Administrative Branch and the many Angels, and Devas, and Nature-Spirits that are involved in all of this Creation.

"And, most importantly, the Archangels and the Ascended Masters are mainly involved in the progress of human souls, so that as many as possible are brought into a State of Enlightenment and consequent Ascension into Realms of Spirit, and so that they will progress in accord with My Cosmic Plan into Ultimate Perfection.

"For, then these human souls will, as Ascended Masters, when ready, then gradually replace the seven Ascended Masters who govern, and control, and guide humanity presently and thereby take their place to take over the responsibility. And they will have the opportunity to progress into higher Stations of My Spiritual Hierarchy throughout other areas of the Omniverse, into different universes and later even different galaxies.

"So you see, My beloved son, it is simply a matter of Spiritual Progression of the various human souls and Ascended Beings into increasing Divine Perfection and so that as many as possible will eventually become as great Gods. Yes, as great Gods who will be responsible for large galaxies and systems of planets throughout My infinite Omniverse. For, there is much space, so-called, that is yet unoccupied or unused. And much space, so-

called, that is yet unoccupied or unused. And much space is yet available, We might say, for many many galaxies, and universes...and yes, millions of planets and stars.

"So, the opportunities that are available and awaiting human souls are, indeed, unending and will lead into ever-more-glorious, more-perfect Levels, Qualities and Expressions of Life and Consciousness in My many Mansions of Spirit and Light. For, My Cosmic Plan of increasing Perfection is to bring forth every worthy human soul to become as a glorious Being of Light...yes, to eventually express as an infinite God expressing all of My Attributes and Qualities as completely as possible throughout My limitless Omniverse!

"This should suffice to answer your question, My beloved son. And thank you for contacting Me again and offering Me this Opportunity to present this Discourse-Lesson to you and to others!"

* * *

About the Author

The author of this rather profound and also prophetic book began to express God in a vocal manner during 1965 after his resignation from the aerospace industry as an engineer. Having been ordained as a minister and also earning a doctorate degree in Divinity, he later discarded his name, plus titles of "Reverend" and "Doctor", when God informed him to simply be named as Jeremiah.

Thereafter, during a 3-year period of seclusion and meditation on a small So. Pacific island, he brought forth a tremendous Revelation from God consisting of 70 discourses, plus a Divine Teaching from the Ascended Master Jesus. These are named and being published as THE AQUARIAN REVELATION and INTO A NEW AGE.

After ending his seclusion, he has been teaching the truths and principles offered in those Divine Teachings to various advanced students. These have been complemented by additional Teachings offered from his personal Communions with God and with various Ascended Beings in the Spiritual Hierarchy.

Also in accord with God's Instruction a CENTER OF UNIVERSAL TRUTH has been established to propagate the Teachings, thus to expand human conşciousness and lead as many as possible into the forthcoming New World and biblically-prophesied "new heaven and new earth". For, as God stated in the AQUARIAN REVELATION "...so as to preserve the Seed of Man on this planet".

From this CENTER OF UNIVERSAL TRUTH located in the high-desert area of Joshua Tree, California, additional Spiritual Teachings are being published in the UNIVERSAL TRUTH magazine, issued monthly, also in correspondence lessons entitled ATTAINING GOD-CONSCIOUSNESS, plus various booklets and newsletters.

THE LOGO
OF
THE CENTER OF UNIVERSAL TRUTH

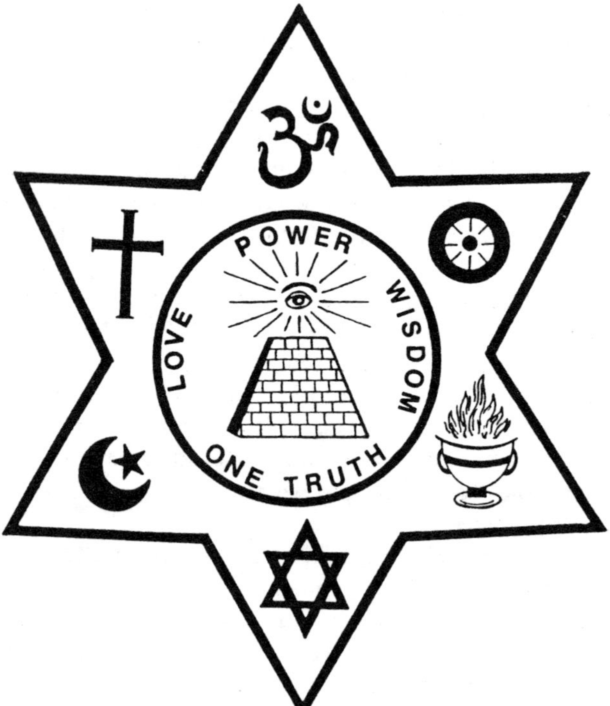

There Is But ONE Truth...
Man Divides it into Many Forms.

CENTER
OF
UNIVERSAL TRUTH

Within the six-pointed Star of David and Solomon's Seal are symbols of the world's six major religions: Christianity, Hinduism, Zoroastrianism, Buddhism, Judaism and Islam.

These six religious symbols encircle the ONE TRUTH of GOD and His three primary Attributes of WISDOM, LOVE and POWER.

At the center of this Star of David with its six religious symbols and God's primary Attributes is the Great Pyramid with the All-seeing Eye of God as shown on the great Seal of the United States of America.

On the principle of these symbols is the CENTER OF UNIVERSAL TRUTH founded to bring forth the ONE TRUTH of God from His All-seeing Eye and primary Attributes of WISDOM, LOVE and POWER to the world's humanity and its religions.

The CENTER OF UNIVERSAL TRUTH is not a typical organization established as a religion, sect, denomination, church, or temple of the world.

As a CENTER OF UNIVERSAL TRUTH, it is a direct Expression, a direct Emanation of the only Source of PURE TRUTH...the CREATOR. Such direct Expression and Emanation of the CREATOR on Earth is a human consciousness, serving as an Instrument, thus establishing a personal Contact and Communion with the CREATOR. In fact, only through such personal

Contact and Communion with the CREATOR can any clergyman or a Spiritual Teacher truly state "*So sayeth the Lord*", as have various Prophets of the past...or to clearly say, as did Jesus, "*The words that I speak, I speak not of myself: but it is the Father within that doeth the works*".

This CENTER is therefore not a worldly organization, but the CREATOR'S direct Expression in and through His Image and Likeness...Man. Through His Spiritual Image and Likeness, the CREATOR brings forth advanced Spiritual Teachings to Earth's humanity during this critical transition period into a New Cycle of Life-expression. Through the CREATOR'S Image and Likeness in a human body serving as His vocal Instrument on Earth, advanced Teachings forming an important part of His New Dispensation are now being offered for preparing Mankind for the now-dawning New Cycle of Life-expression and its biblically-prophesied new heaven and new earth.

* * *